Unseen Chains: Culture of Shame in Arab Society

An In-depth Examination of Social Control in Arab Communities.

Dr. Fatma Al-Zahraa

Contents

Foreword

A wide range of practices and standards—both positive and negative, rational and irrational—shape our daily lives. These practices and standards have a significant impact on our actions and behaviors. This study aims to examine shame, one of the most pervasive and common concepts in our daily lives. It forms the basis of many of the norms and standards that govern our lives and is noticeable in various settings such as households, schools, workplaces, and public spaces. The concept of shame imposes a set of rules, standards, and codes of conduct that dictate what is acceptable in society. This includes guidelines around topics that should not be discussed, words that should not be used, boundaries that should not be crossed, and standards of cultural expectations that dictate which parts of the body should be covered or concealed. Members of society are expected to follow these rules and norms in order to preserve social order and cohesion.

Although the concept of shame is clearly significant, it is not formed in society independently and objectively, as if it were a principle that must not be deviated from. Instead, it is notable that in various cases, this concept is used to articulate the interests of one class over another or to elevate the status of certain members of society over others. The problem with the study is the examination of the social use of the concept of shame and its correlation to the idea of "power." Here, "power" refers to the ability to influence and direct behavior, implying that the concept can be employed as a tool by certain individuals to establish their status and reinforce their authority through the implementation of a set of mandates and restrictions.

Once we delve into the social environment, we will find many practices that depict manifestations of power that are evident across various fields and domains, such as age, gender, and class. These practices are evident in the power dynamics between individuals, such as the way elders exercise authority over younger people by dictating rules of conversation, determining who is allowed to speak and who should listen, and controlling body language and behavior through imposed rules. It is also evident in the power that men exercise over women, which forces women to submit to the authority of their father, husband, or brother, even if the man is younger than the woman. This power imposes certain prohibitions and restrictions, determining a woman's dress code, ability to make choices, freedom of speech, and relationships with others. These restrictions are a form of social control over women. It is also apparent in the relationship between a leader and those they lead, as well as in the relationship between the wealthy and the poor. In addition, there are certain prohibitions and topics related to shame that reveal inequalities and social distinctions. There is another manifestation of power that exists in the symbolic power that society exercises over its members, where individuals also exert it over themselves. As a member of society with a certain status, an individual may want to act freely and spontaneously, but they will carefully consider their actions and perhaps avoid them altogether due to fear of how society will react, how they will be perceived, and whether their image will be tarnished in the eyes of others. These fears represent forms of power and oppression in society, which create a fertile ground for the concept of shame to thrive.

The problem of the study is limited to the following question: What determines what is considered shameful or wrong in daily life, and what are the forms of power inherent in it?

A) The concept of shame:

Idiomatically, I haven't been able to find a precise scientific definition of shame in the various social studies that I've referred to, except for a concept described in a study by Frederic Maatouk. Maatouk defined shame in that study by stating that: Shame is a very relative social concept that is based on interrupting certain body movements on the grounds that they oppose to the formal pattern approved by the knowledge-holders and authority figures in the social structure. (Frederic Maatouk, 1982, p. 152). In the paragraph immediately following his definition, Maatouk clarified that the 'certain body movements' he referred to were specific to women. As a result, Maatouk limited the definition of shame to the interruption of particular women-specific body movements because they go against the formal pattern that knowledge holders and authority figures in the social structure have approved. This limitation makes Maatouk's definition inconsistent with this study because the definition, in this form, only includes a small subset of it. In contrast, this study aims to examine the concept of shame within the context of various social practices in everyday life, requiring the concept to be characterized by a sense of generality and free from any preconceived ideology to ensure the necessary objectivity. Additionally, it should provide a comprehensive framework for examining daily life situations.

So I suggest defining the concept of shame as "deviating from what society deems correct, with regard to values, customs and traditions, and behavioral standards." Consequently, this definition would entail that the word "shame" will primarily be aimed at ending wrong practices and adhering to proper behaviors that are consistent with society's values and behavioral standards. The number of restrictions and prohibitions placed on one's body, speech, and interpersonal relationships determines the procedural definition of shame. Such prohibitions are imposed on the body (such as the rules governing walking and movement, standing and sitting, and the prohibitions imposed on dress in terms of its color, specifications, and quality). As for the prohibitions imposed on the language, they are represented in the voice volume, the quality and manner of speech, the culture of silence, and the taboo topics. As for the prohibitions imposed on the relationship with the other, they are represented in the limits of the relationship boundaries with the opposite sex, the relationship boundaries between the young and the old, and the superior-subordinate relationship boundaries.

B) The concept of everyday life:

The necessity of human existence or the unrestricted state of being, is everyday life. This state of existence comprises several elements, such as the material living environment in which individuals live and the cultural environment that organizes the living environment and defines its relations with the broader structure. There are also forms of material and cultural exchange that establish a connection with the lives of individuals and facilitate their reproduction. Finally, some forms of intervention contribute to reproducing everyday life when aspects of material and cultural exchange fail to do so. (Ahmed Zayed, 1992, p. 20). According to Wolfgang Wagner (2005, 23), daily life is the real, lived experience through which individuals acquire their basic capabilities, beliefs, emotions, forms of behavior, and practices that enable them to interact with each other in various places, including home, street, school, club, workplace, and means of transportation.

C) The concept of Power[1]

Conventionally, power is the exercise of an action over human behavior, meaning the ability to influence the behavior and direct it toward the goals and objectives determined by those who can impose their will (Fardon, 1985). It is also defined as the ability of an individual or a group to exercise power and influence over others, pressure them, monitor and control them, discipline their behavior and influence their actions, and direct their efforts towards certain perspectives

---

1. It is worth noting that the translation of this concept in some Lebanese texts has the connotation of "Authority". In the meanwhile, the translation of the same concept in the Egyptian text is linked to "Power", to distinguish it from the word (authority), which means the legitimate use of force.

in order to achieve specific goals and values, whether with their consent and conviction or by force and coercion. (Alsayyid Abd al-Hamid Al-Zayyat, 1990, p. 117: 118). Power is also defined as not only being exercised when someone forces others to do something but also when they force them to think, feel, and believe in a certain thing and to value certain things highly while devaluing others in a way that makes that person subordinate to the former in determining their interests and priorities. (Michael Parenti, 1978, p. 42) There are two types of power: direct power and indirect power. Direct power is defined as the ability to coerce and force someone to do something, so that they become unable to do anything else contrary to what they have been directed to do. This definition of direct power was commonly known as the definition of power in American sociology to the end of the sixties. And it is still widely used in social psychology. For example, in 1964, Blou defined power as the ability to impose one's will on others and oppress their resistance to achieve certain goals. As for indirect power, it is the ability to shape the lives of others through the use of symbols, without resorting to direct control (discipline). The researchers noticed the role of culture in these two definitions of power. This is due to the fact that culture is considered a field to grow power relations, a source to create oppression, and a medium for power relations through symbols that are based on cultural exemptions and social inequality (Lamont Michele, 1989). In the context of this study, the procedural definition of power is defined in terms of cultural power, which encompasses customs, traditions, and conventions. Those who have the ability to influence others through these cultural elements represent this power.

D) The Concept of Representation:

The concept of representation is an accumulation of values, ideas, beliefs, and practices shared by members of a society (Smelser). N, 2001). Goffman defined representations as the roles or expectations that others have about our behavior in certain circumstances. These representations can be thought of as scripts that we act upon and are shaped by the surrounding social and cultural environment. (Goffman. E, 1959).

E) Representations of Power

They are the individual's presence and his actual performance in life, with the help of some material and symbolic mechanisms, in order to establish his power and status in society.

Two tools will be used to collect field material.

a) The first tool: Observation

Observation is an important tool in identifying practices that are related to the concepts of shame, way of performing, sound volume, and type and quality of clothing. In addition, observation is a critical tool when it comes to recording silent situations that depend on gestures, looks of approval and resentment, and body movement and its implications.

b) The second tool: The record sheet of daily life situations[2]

This tool aims to investigate the realistic representations of individuals, where recorded conversations explain the stance people take in everyday life and how they represent themselves in terms of strength, submission, and resistance through their position in the social environment. It also shows how the concept of shamefulness is formed in the spontaneous practices of individuals in everyday life through their native tongue, volume of voice, clothing, signs, and gestures. These conversations take place in any place, such as the house, the street, gardens, cafes, means of transportation, and workplaces. A description of the participants in the situation is provided in terms of their education level,

---

2. Refer to Ahmed Zayed: The Discourse of Everyday Life, Dar Al Qiraa lil Jameei, first edition 1992, p. 24.

profession, social class, age, and gender. This study is conducted without seeking the name of the respondent or any personal information about them, which may result in deviating from the objective of the research from its framework. As the objective of the research is to know the interactions of individuals in daily life situations spontaneously, without the researcher's interference in directing the conversation towards a certain perspective, The topic of the conversation must be recorded in the same language that is used in daily life, including common proverbs and sayings. This record sheet of situations should be divided into:

- a) Data on the situation (where it occurred and who recorded it)

- b) Data on the participants in the situation (place of residence - number - gender - profession - level of education)

- c) The topic of the shame

- d) The contexts of use

- c) The strength stances in conversations

- f) The weakness stances

- g) The resistance stances

The situation sample:

A sample of situations was randomly selected, with a focus on topics related to shame, whether related to norms, traditions, cultural values, or topics in which the word "shame" is mentioned in various contexts. A number of situations that do not align with the research objective are excluded, resulting in a final selection of 420 situations from everyday life in Egypt. These situations encompass diverse social contexts, including poor neighborhoods, rich neighborhoods, public spaces, clubs, and different modes of transportation.

1

Topics of Shame in Everyday Life

I: Shame and the Ritualization of Life

A ritual, in its simplest sense, means every activity that an individual performs continuously or repeatedly (Roland A., 1987, 72: 74). Daily life produces a set of rituals and practices related to speech patterns and rules, clothing style and appearance, manner of speaking, sitting, standing, walking, and other rituals. The ritualistic shame is a set of commands and prohibitions that are related to the individual's performance in life and determine how he speaks, moves, and interacts with others.

Upon my observation of everyday life situations, I found that rituals are primarily prominent in the lives of the middle class. This could be attributed to the fact that rituals serve as the main means through which this class presents itself to others. Therefore, they are careful to perform these rituals to maintain the desired image they wish to portray, which includes setting certain restrictions and limitations on their practices. As a result, the topics related to shame that are associated with rituals are abundant, reaching a percentage of 34% of the situations. These have been summarized into two main topics: body and movement rituals, and language rituals.

a.   Body and movement rituals

Topics related to physical rituals and movement restrictions accounted for as much as 70% of the total. These rituals include actions such as getting up, sitting down, going to bed, waking up and moving. It also involves showing or hiding certain parts of the body, which is considered one of the most important culturally influenced rituals that defines the ideal body image associated with dignity. One of the main themes of ritual-related stigma is when the body loses its dignity through movement, playfulness, recklessness, or indulgence.

For example, some people would perform some rituals that cause them to lose their body control; thus they would do unaccountable or reckless actions, such as playing, children destroying things, and eating in outdoors. Similarly, certain practices performed by the body can have a negative impact on the image of the person in the eyes of others, such as dancing, removing certain clothing items, engaging in biological activities in public places, visiting nightclubs, and getting pregnant at a later age. These are all the body rituals and their related topics of shame. But, what about the relationship of one's body with the bodies of others?

Indeed, there are rituals related to the relationship of one's body with other bodies and the topics of shame that result from that relationship. For example:

- A man jostling a woman in a means of transportation.

- A woman sitting closely next to a man in public transportation.

- The man walks ahead of the woman.

- A young man crosses his legs in the presence of his father.

- A man not offering an elderly woman his seat on the train.

- A wife beating her husband.

- A mother-in-law kissing her daughter's groom.

- Spouses caressing each other in front of their children.

- Shaking hands as a form of greeting between unrelated men and women.

- A man greeting a seated woman.

- A woman sitting in the passenger seat of the car and a man sitting in the back seat.

The body's rituals and movements reveal the nature of this body's relationship with other bodies and the nature of the culture determining the form of that relationship. The prevailing culture imposes kinetic rituals in the relationship between a son and his father, characterized by reverence and appreciation. Similarly, in the relationship between a man and a woman, culture imposes rituals of reservation and respect.

b.   Language rituals

30% of the ritual topics are about language rituals and their associated topics of shame. The topics of shame related to language rituals are categorized into three categories.

1) Voice volume:
- Laughing out loud in the street (outdoors).
- A woman's loud voice.
- The boy resembles the girl in crying and having a soft voice.

2) Language contexts
Young children talking in the presence of adults.
- A girl talking to her male colleague on the phone.
- A husband insulting his wife.
- A man insulting his colleague.

3) The content of conversations

- Jokes between males and females.
- Talking about sex.
- Using offensive language in public (outdoors).

II - Shame and Rebellion:

The dominant culture enforces a set of customs and traditions that mold individuals into stereotyped forms. And thus, breaking these molds becomes an act of rebellion against those traditions. The topics associated with rebellion in everyday situations are numerous, comprising approximately 25% of the topics of shame. As a result, I have decided to categorize them into three types, namely: Gender Rebellion, age-related rebellion, and class-related rebellion.

a) Gender Rebellion

This type includes topics that are related to women's rebellion, comprising 53% of the topics of rebellion. It exposes the stereotype of submission, obedience, and meekness that the prevailing culture molds women into. Breaking such stereotype is considered a topic of rebellion. The following topics represent this type:

- A woman coming home late at night.
- A divorced woman living by herself.
- A girl disobeying her parent/guardian.
- A woman commanding her husband.
- Disobedience of a wife to her husband.
- A girl's marriage without the approval of her family.
- A girl's engagement to a man younger than her.
- A lady speaking in the presence of men.
- A widow wearing bright colors.

And this isn't the list of women's rebellious acts that would bring shame upon them. But it also includes other acts of rebellion like seeking their right to education, work, and choosing their life partner. Some topics of women's rebellion against society are:"

- An educated girl refusing to marry an uneducated relative.

- A woman divorcing her husband through Khula (refers to a woman initiating the dissolution of her marriage by requesting a divorce from her husband. It is a legal term used in the context of marriage and divorce in Arabic-speaking countries).

- Remarriage of a widow after the recent death of her husband.

- A wife working and gaining income higher than her husband's.

b) Age-related rebellion:

By this, I mean the acts of rebellion of the young against the old, and the many related topics of shame. This type constitutes 31% of the topics of rebellion, and its examples include:

- A young person calling an elder without titles.

- A young person arguing with an elder.

- A young person blaming an elder.

- A student expressing her opinion in front of her male teacher.

- A student not leaving a distance between him and his teacher.

- Refusing the son to comply with his father's desire to join a specific college.

- A son crossing his leg in the presence of his father.

From the previous topics, we can conclude that the topic of rebellion does not just stop at the extent of assaulting and insulting the elders, but also reaches to expressing personal opinion in front of their elders, discussing it, or even simply blaming them. Furthermore, these topics also highlight the relatively young age of those who rebel or show disrespect towards their elders, often occurring during their university years or slightly before or after that. However, the following topics provide other examples and instances of age-related acts of rebellion that are done by people who may have reached the stage of adulthood. However, their practices and actions towards their elders still remain a topic of rebellion, thus indicating the concept of the "absolute young", and the "absolute old". A young person remains young as long as an elder exists. For example:

- A young person will start hosting the elder in social events.

- A forty-five-year-old man smokes cigarettes in front of his uncle. His uncle scolds him, "Shame on you, you are such an insolent brat."

- A woman asks her aunt about her share of the inheritance from her grandmother, which makes the aunt angry, and she tells her, "Don't you ever cross the line when you talk to me!"

- A father refuses to allow his children to question or discuss his behavior, seeing it as a rebellion against his authority.

- "An uncle denounces his middle-aged nephew for disposing of his own properties by selling them without consulting him, saying to him, 'Whoever has no elder relative, must seek one. You should have consulted me first.'"

These topics are not very different from the previous ones, except for the age of the rebel. In these cases, the acts of rebellion occur during middle age, which is considered a stage of maturity or adulthood. However, the person engaging in rebellion may still be seen as young by their elders, who do not tolerate such defiance of authority. And in case he resisted it, he will be considered a rebel in their eyes, even if he was asking them for his legal rights, such as inheritance, for example. This confirms what I've concluded: the young person will always remain young as long as the elders exist.

c) Class-related rebellion:

This type represents 16% of the topics of rebellion. It's clearly evident in the superior-subordinate relationship, which is represented in the following situations:

- A school teacher confronts her superior at work, verbally accusing him of being unjust.

- A school teacher argues with the principal of the school, "I dare you if someone can explain lessons like me." He tells her off, "You must address your superior in a much better way."

- A service worker in a public organization refuses to bring breakfast to an employee who requested it, saying, 'Why didn't you ask earlier? I just finished delivering breakfast to your colleagues.' As a result, the employee files a complaint with the manager, citing inappropriate behavior from the worker.

- An employee was fooling around with his colleagues and laughing loudly. When the manager heard him, he reprimanded him, "Where do you think you are? Do respect the place you are in!"

III - Shame and personal flaws:

Personal flaws are a topic of shame, and they comprise about 9% of the topics of shame in everyday life. This topic deals with moral (personal) and physical flaws in a person. There is a group of moral flaws that are related to the essence of personality, which include:

- Gossip.
- Disclosure of secrets.
- Breaking promises.
- Driving wedges among people.
- A man's weak personality.
- A woman's strong personality.
- A person praising himself.
- A girl's delay in marriage.
- A man's unemployment.

As for physical flaws, they are related to the appearance of a person, such as:

- A woman's thinness (underweight).
- Obesity.
- Curly/kinky hair.
- Ugliness.
- Dark skin color.

- Short stature / extreme tallness.

These are some of the moral (personal) and physical flaws that are related to the personality of the individual. By reviewing them, the following can be concluded:

1. All members of society share some common shameful (disgraceful) traits, whether they are male or female. Gossip, aiming at driving wedges among people, and disclosure of secrets are all flaws that can be committed by both men and women, and they are not gender-exclusive flaws.

2. In general, a trait is not considered a flaw by nature; Rather, it becomes so through its association with the other. A woman, for example, is not flawed if she is educated, wealthy, brilliant, or tall. However, all of these traits can turn into explicit flaws when linked to and compared to her other half. Likewise, a man cannot be flawed if he is short, handsome, or in his young age. But that could be a disadvantage against him when associated with his other half. Presenting some examples from daily life situations would prove the validity of this argument:

After marriage, a husband prevented his wife, who excelled academically, from completing her postgraduate studies at her college, due to the fact that he was a classmate of hers at the same college, stating that, "What would people say? His wife is higher than him in education!"

A girl refuses to marry a guy younger than her, saying, "I'm not going to marry a boy this young!" Another girl rejects the other guy because he is more attractive than her, saying, 'Who is the man here and who is the woman? Girls are hitting on him while he's walking with me!"

A woman being taller than a man is considered a flaw. Likewise, if she is richer than him.

The boy is born with attractive features, fair skin, and smooth hair, while his sister has dark skin and curly hair. The family remarks, "If only the girl had been born with these desirable traits instead of her brother..." He is a man and he cannot be ashamed about anything."

The girl outperforms her brother academically, as he struggles with his studies. Their parents scold him, saying, "How disgraceful! Your sister, who is a girl, is doing better than you. What a failure you are!"

The traditional societal roles assigned to females often limit them to specific functions, such as marriage, childbearing, and child-rearing. If a woman seeks education, she is not necessarily expected to be a genius or excel academically. As for the role that society assigns to males often includes expectations of academic, financial, physical, and intellectual excellence, while excluding traits considered feminine, such as beauty. This trait is supposed to be exclusive to females, as it is believed to increase their chances of marriage.

3) In addition, society turns some flawed traits into advantages in favor of men. These traits are considered disadvantages and flaws in a woman's personality, yet, they are regarded as the pinnacle of manhood in men. For example:

a) Flaws in a man's character

- An old man dying his hair black: "He should respect his age, he looks like a clown, it's obvious he's trying to hide his true appearance."

- An unemployed man: "He takes his pocket money from his wife."

- A man breaks his promise: "He's not a man of his word and cannot be trusted!"

– A man with weak personality: "A spineless man! His wife controls him."

- A kind-hearted man: "A halfwit!"

All these flaws in a man's personality are not deemed flaws in a woman's personality. Rather, society may find them advantages that a woman can and need to possess (to be kind-hearted, with weak personality and unemployed) as long as she remains under the guardianship of a man, who is responsible for her and for meeting her material needs. And since she is an incompetent and incapacitated being, what's wrong with her when she break her promise? And in order for a woman to complement her qualities to the best, she must be beautiful. Therefore, society has no qualms for a woman to adorn herself and dye her greying hair, unlike men.

b) Flaws in a woman's character

- A girl breaking off her engagement more than once.

- A Divorcee's marriage more than once.

- A married woman becoming pregnant at a later age.

– A man proposed to a woman who is very thin. However, his family made derogatory comments about the girl, asking why he chose her and suggesting that she may have come from a famine-stricken region.

- A single lady who is over thirty-five and has not been married yet. A mother argues with her son who intends to propose to this lady. The mother said to him, "She is a spinster, my son! She is old for marriage. What compels you to marry a spinster?"

- A strong-willed woman

- A bold girl

- "A girl who works as a conductor on a public transportation bus, wears a shirt and trousers, and puts money between her fingers; she calls out to the passengers at every station very boldly, while everyone looks at her with surprise and astonishment."

These previously mentioned flaws in a woman's personality do not represent any problem for a man. The man is obligated to work independently, and be of strong personality. He is not flawed by either being a divorcee, or breaking off his engagement multiple times. His age is not a disadvantage when it comes to marriage and reproduction.

IV. Shame and sex:

One the topics of shame is sex, and all its related perceptions, beliefs, or practices, whether they encourage inclination towards it, or reluctance against it. Upon reflecting on the sex-related topics of shame within the context of the everyday life situations, I found that they revolve around two main topics. The first of which is women's inclination towards it, while the second revolves around men's reluctance against it. The aforementioned topics are described below.

A) Women's inclination: women hold a significant position in our societies when it comes to the topic of sex, and they are often subjected to scrutiny. As a result, women face numerous prohibitions and restrictions imposed by various traditions and customs that begin from birth and continue throughout their lives, with power being successively wielded over them by their father, brother, and husband. As a result, sex becomes one of the primary taboos for women, and it is deemed scandalous or shameful for a woman to show an inclination towards such topics, including matters related to love, for instance. Society regards itself safe and secure as long as women keep their eyes wide shut on this aspect. And it would be the utmost shame when their eyes are wide opens on this other world. So, let's reflect upon some everyday life situations to see how women's inclination towards sex is considered a topic of shame.

- A group of female employees talking about sex with jokes and innuendos, but when their colleague, Miss, enters the room, they fall silent and say, 'Just because the girl is here and shouldn't hear this conversation.'

- A family is watching a romantic scene on TV. And when the daughter came to join them, the father went to turn off the TV.

- A man ends his engagement with a girl after they kissed, expressing doubts about her fidelity by saying, 'How can I be certain that this hasn't happened with others, or that it didn't happen with someone else before me?'

- A husband prevents his wife from knowing about her divorced and liberated friend.

- A mother advises her daughter, the bride, on her wedding day to be negative and unresponsive towards her husband so as not to be misunderstood.

- In a parent-teacher meeting, a student's mother advocated the need for teaching sex-education in schools, and she was met with the rejection and disapproval of the attendees.

It is evident from the above that when women show inclination towards anything related to sex, society starts to be wary of, disapproving and concerned with such inclination. Therefore, it begins to put restrictions and prohibitions to limit and suppress their behavior. It is considered shameful and disgraceful for a girl to talk about sex or engage in romantic relationships. If any compromising or insolent situation occurs in her relationship with her fiancé, she and her family will be blamed, with her family being stigmatized for not raising her well. That's why society tends to be wary and suspicious of a girl who gets engaged more than once. Questions may be raised about her perceived flaws or reasons for not getting married earlier. And what were the limits or boundaries in her previous engagement? All of these questions reflect society's concerns about women's sexual behavior. Therefore, it is common to see a mother advising her daughter on her wedding day to be passive with her husband, in order to avoid further questions or doubts about her sexual experience.

B) Men's reluctance: On one hand, the prevailing culture deems a woman's inclination towards sex as shameful. On the other hand, society views a man's reluctance towards sex as shameful." This is manifested in making the man the primary actor in the relationship with the other party (woman). Thus, we find that he is the one who can love, confess his love boldly, and choose whoever he wants to marry. This is in addition to his ability to openly boast about his past multiple relationships and experiences, as well as his wide range of sexual knowledge. So, any reluctance or failure in fulfilling his previous role is considered a matter of shame. Everyday life is full of situations that demonstrate and reveal this issue, including:

- A man undergoing a medical examination before marriage.

- A young man who doesn't have a relationship with a girl.

- A man buying sexual enhancers:

"A man walked into a pharmacy and asked the pharmacist to bring him (the famous) sexual enhancement pills. When the pharmacist was about to get him the pills, the man's neighbor burst into the pharmacy. They then greeted each other. His neighbor asks him, "Are you okay? I hope you feel better soon. What medicine do you buy? " The man answered, "Don't worry! I just have a cold and I need some flu medicine." Then he signaled to the pharmacist discreetly, away from his neighbor, not to bring him his order.

- A man not boasting about his multiple relationships with women.

Unresponsiveness of some men to sex jokes told by their peers:

A group of men were telling sexually suggestive jokes loudly, but when one of their colleagues scolded them to keep it down so that no one at work would overhear, one of them replied, "What's the big deal? Isn't this just typical guy talk? Or are you not one of us?"

These examples reveal to us that the topics of sex for men and the disgraceful/shameful issues they represent, are the topics that primarily affect their manhood; which is an entity that should not be touched, marred, flawed, or disgraced/shamed. He is not easily convinced of the idea of undergoing a medical examination before or after marriage to ensure fertility, as he considers himself completely free from any flaws. Similarly, parents may have concerns about their young son not establishing any relationship with a girl due to fear of medical obstacles. Anything that poses a threat to their masculinity is practiced in complete secrecy, such as going to a urologist or purchasing sexual enhancers. To avoid undermining this masculinity, a man must openly promote it with courage and pride. He announces to his peers about his multiple relationships with women, his youthful adventures of flirting with girls, and freely indulges in sexual jokes and discussions without hesitation.

VI- Bordering on femininity:

Upon reflecting on everyday situations, it became evident to me how closely linked this topic is to the previous one, which is sex. For men, sex is often their primary concern and a yardstick by which they are evaluated. Any compromise to the concept of masculinity is considered delicate and can be a source of shame. Therefore, it's natural that when a man exhibits behavior that deviates from traditional masculine norms and borders on the feminine side, it may trigger concerns and anxieties, leading to more topics of shame. In the following examples, we will provide instances where individuals may feel they are bordering on femininity.

- A discussion between a group of men about helping their wives in the household chores. One of them says, "The Prophet (PBUH) commanded us to treat women well, and he was helping his wives at home." Another man replied to him, opposing him, "But it's shameful for a man to wash and cook. A man will always be a man. And a woman will still be a woman." And then another one said sarcastically, 'Excuse me, guys, I have to leave early today because I have laundry to do."

- A man scolds his son, "Shame on you! You must not act like women. Your voice should be deeper. Stop being soft and acting sissy. A man must be tough." When boy cried because his father reprimanded him, his father said, "Men don't cry. What have you lifted for girls?"

- A father berates his son after seeing him holding a small doll while playing with his sister. He tells him, "A boy plays with a ball or a gun, not a doll, like girls. I'm warning you not to play with a doll again."

- A boy went to a store to buy candy, but the saleswoman didn't hear him the first time. He stood on the street for a long time until a man came out of the store and asked him, "Why didn't you ask for what you wanted multiple times?" The child replied, "I'm waiting for her to finish her work." The man responded mockingly, "Are you shy like girls? It's the first time I see a man feeling shy! You are a man, aren't you?"

- A man who has a soft voice and is not loud, his colleagues mockingly nickname him after a woman.

- A rural man refuses to mention his wife's name in public and considers everything related to her as shameful. He refers to her as 'the family' or 'the children'.

- The man feeling pained when he is wounded.

- A man resembling women due to his weak personality.

- A child in the primary school prevents his mother from inquiring about him or dropping him off at school, saying to her, "My classmates call me a baby and ask if I'm mama's little girl because you drop me off at school."

These examples reveal men's concern and embarrassment when bordering on femininity. But are men the only ones who get anxious and concerned when bordering on femininity? Or does women share these concerns? Perhaps the following situations will answer this question:

- A mother refuses to be called and referred to by her daughter's name, and instead asks to be called and referred to by her son's name.

- A mother calls her son with feminine nicknames as a form of pampering, but the child's grandmother rebukes her and warns her not to call him that again. The grandmother insists that the child should be brought up like a tough man from his early childhood.

- A mother forbids her teenage daughter from applying lipstick, telling her that it's too soon for her to do so, as lipstick is meant for much older women only.

- A girl loudly called her friend at the university by her name, but her friend scolded her, saying, "You shouldn't call me by my name, it's really embarrassing! Now everyone knows my name."

- A veiled woman in a bus is holding a lovely little girl. A woman sitting beside her admires the child and says to the mother, "Your daughter is adorable." The mother argued, "You mean she's a big trouble. I gave birth to a trouble! Girls are troubles. We are burdened with their upbringing and their morals."

The examples provided clearly illustrate how a culture that prioritizes masculinity over femininity can also affect women. It may lead them to view themselves as something that needs to be covered and hidden, as well as feeling ashamed and flawed, while perceiving masculinity as the ideal standard. Whenever a woman gets closer to expressing her femininity, she becomes more acutely aware of her shortcomings and flaws. It becomes a fault for her to mention her own name, so she compensates by using "Mrs. So-and-So" or "Mother of So-and-So" instead. She perceives herself as something that should be concealed and not revealed, considering it shameful to speak loudly or exhibit any signs of womanhood, such as speaking or applying makeup, at a young age, as if it is reserved for grown women only.

VII- Minimalist consumption

Minimalist consumption means consuming as much as needed without resorting to extravagant and ostentatious consumption. This type of consumption is inclined to moderation and rationing (saving). Consumer culture is characterized by ostentation, where consumption is often driven by the need to display oneself publicly. The more an individual consumes, the higher their perceived prestige and status. Consumption becomes a way for individuals to showcase and present themselves to others. An individual's body plays a prominent role in such display through the quality of clothes, perfumes, and types of jewelry women wear. Families also compete in showing off themselves by highlighting the size of their consumption; It starts with the exaggerated dowries, bridal jewelry, furniture, cars, feasts, and other forms of conspicuous consumption. Hence, for a culture that promotes conspicuous consumption, advocating saving and minimalist consumption can be considered a topic of shame. Let us reflect on some of our everyday practices that are related to this topic.

-     A woman feels embarrassed to ask about the price of an item she wants to buy, justifying it by saying, "The sellers judge people based on their appearance. If I ask them about the price upfront, they will know that I am not a frequent buyer, and it will be a waste of time. That's why I need to have plenty of money with me before making a purchase, and even more."

-     A discussion between two families, where the bride's family set a certain price for their daughter's bridal jewelry that is rival those of her relatives and with their social status. But the groom's family thinks it's exaggerated.

-     A fiancé and his bride come to an agreement not to have a wedding ceremony, opting instead to purchase practical, simple, modern furniture and save the money that would have been spent on the ceremony for future use. However, their decision is met with disapproval from their families. The bride's mother refuses, saying, "Do you want people to mock and gossip about us? They will ask why we didn't have a wedding ceremony and why you got married quietly. And what about your practical furniture? What will you say if someone visits your home? Are you living in a summer resort now?"

Among the topics of shame are the topics of consumption that are associated with food, its quality and quantity, including:

- A housewife invited three friends of the family to dinner, but she prepared a large feast with multiple dishes that would be enough to feed twenty people.

She chose to provide excessive quantities of food that would likely go to waste and be thrown away later, so as not to be labeled as stingy or overly frugal.

- A girl and her friend from the countryside traveled to Cairo to purchase some necessities. While in Cairo, they visited the girl's relative at his workplace to check on him. After the meeting, he offered to give them a ride to the nearest location on his way back home. However, they refused and left on their own. The friend commented, "By the way, your relative seems stingy and disrespectful. He didn't even bother to invite you for lunch. If he were to visit our town, it would be shameful if he left without eating. We would have been rushing around to prepare the food."

- A mother scolded her young son when he told her at a relative's house, "Mommy, I'm hungry." The hostess understood and started preparing food for him, but the mother refused and said, "I swear, you don't need to do so. He's not hungry. I don't know what's gotten into him, he just ate before we came here. He never asks for food, and we always have to coax him to eat."

- A man used to purchase large quantities of fruits, often buying multiple types of fruits. After his children got married, he and his wife were left alone in their house. His wife was surprised to find out that he still bought the same excessive amount of fruit. She told him, "You shouldn't have spent so much money! We only need one kilogram of each fruit, considering it's just the two of us now, and the excess will go to waste and end up in the trash." He replied, "You know that the fruit seller has known us for a long time. I would feel embarrassed to only buy one kilogram from him. What would he think of me then?"

2

Shame Uses (Shaming) in Everyday Life

I- Shame and contradictions of mean-ing:

Initially, the research settled on a proposed definition of shame, which indicates that it is used to end wrong practices and promote correct practices. According to this definition, shame serves as society's form of justice that corrects mistakes in order to uphold the values and cultural standards of the society. And thus, does our use of shame in our daily lives always align with what I've mentioned? I leave it to everyday life situations to answer this question.

- The employee persuaded his co-worker that he could travel abroad for work through an external labor recruitment agency owned by someone he knows, in exchange for a fee of fifteen thousand pounds. The co-worker gave the employee the amount without receiving a receipt, as he trusted him and believed that he would be able to travel soon. Several months went by, and there were no signs of the possibility of traveling. Every time his co-worker asked about the travel date and visa, he would procrastinate and say, "Just be patient; I haven't been able to meet the man yet." The passage of time stretched on, and the debtor grew increasingly concerned. He approached his colleague and expressed, "If the travel plans are going to be further delayed, there is no guarantee of safety in life, and it is my right to protect my interests. Could you please provide me with a receipt for the amount I gave you?" His colleague responded with intense emotion, catching the attention of their fellow coworkers, saying, "How dare you say such a thing!" Is that what we've been up to now! Shame on you man! What receipt are you talking about? Do you not trust me?! I will even sell my home furniture and return your money to you. How could you say so to me!?" So the colleagues turned against the debtor, scolding him for his unreasonable request, until he went ashamed of his request.

If we examined this situation closely, we will find that the word (shame) has great power and influence. The money owner legitimately asked to secure his rights after he faced procrastination in fulfilling his wish to travel and his colleague who took the money refused to give him his legitimate right. However, he cannot expressly refuse that request. Otherwise, he would be guilty in the eyes of his colleague, which is something that could make the rest of the colleagues stand against him in solidarity with their debtor colleague. By then, things had gone against his wishes. As a result, he employed the word "shame" as a tool that shifted the balance in his favor. It transformed him from being viewed as the one who took his colleague's money and denied his rightful claim, to being seen as a victim. The debtor's lack of trust and wrongful perception of him as deceitful were grave mistakes that were exposed through the power of shame.

- An employee who has been causing problems and disturbance with her colleagues at work. When her manager was fed up with her multiple problems, she decided to file a complaint to hold her accountable and transfer her to another place. The employee wanted to deter her manager from her intent, but she was unable to do so. She went to the deputy, cried and reminded her that she had been working in this place for thirty years, where she started as a young employee, and with her the manager and the deputy who were appointed some years ahead of her. The deputy went to admonish the manager, saying, "It would be a shame to forsake an old employee... I can't believe it easy for you to get over this long relation. What did she do? I mean, just usual problems with some new employees. Overall, if I must transfer someone, you should choose one of the new employees and leave the old one." The manager complied with her colleague's orders and transferred another employee for the sake of the old camaraderie.

Perhaps this situation is a stark example of the standards' conflict and absurdity. We can observe that the standards designed to punish wrongdoers and reward those who do right have vanished, replaced by other standards that may punish the doer of good and reward the wrongdoer, solely for the sake of old camaraderie. The only mistake made by the newly appointed employee was not having a long history of camaraderie with them at work. As a result, she had to bear the consequences of the trouble caused by the troublesome employee.

- A mother visits her young son's school to collect his exam results. The mother had previously been employed as a teacher at this school but was later transferred to another school. She is acquainted with most of the teachers at this school. When she learned of her son's failure in most of his subjects, and realized that her son would have to repeat his academic year once again, she complained to the school principal, lashing out, "Shame on you! You fail my son, and you know he's my child. What a shame! How could you do this to me!" The principal comforts her and reassures her that she will take action. Therefore, the principal rushed to the teachers in charge of marking the tests and those in charge of giving the results and admonished them, saying, "Come on, folks! What happened to this boy is a total shame. Our colleague's son must be dealt with in a generous way." So they modified the boy's final results and was moved from the lists of those who failed, to the lists of those who passed the tests, after changing the result sheets.

This mother took advantage of the previous camaraderie to shame her colleagues in order to secure the success of her son and get him something he didn't deserve.

- A man approached his relative, who held a high position, to request employment for his son who had recently graduated with just a "Pass" grade average, at a bank. The relative responded, "I'm sorry, Hajj. Your son must have at least a 'very good' grade average, and there are other conditions, such as proficiency in a foreign language, that must be met. So, how could we appoint him? What can I say in favor of him?" The man answered, "It would be a shame if your refused my request. I've high hopes in you. It would be disappointing if you couldn't help me, especially since we are relatives. Can you treat my son like your own son?" His relative replied, "Ok, Hajj. I'll do my best."

This situation is not much different from the previous one, as both of them are using their familial relation to achieve an unjust goal, relying on shame to accomplish it. This indicates a clear contradiction between the meaning of shame and its practice.

A man offered a ride to a police corporal in his car on a highway, as they were heading towards the entrance of the corporal's village. When the driver tried to fasten his seat belt, the police corporal stopped him and said with strong disapproval, "Shame on you! I'm sitting right next to you. I swear you wouldn't need to fasten your seatbelt! Come on! Who dares to talk to you while I am sitting next to you?"

- A young man brags to his friends about his ability to obtain phone numbers from girls and establish relationships with them. One of his friends warned him this would be a tough job for him and assures him that the girl is hard to get. The young man replied, "Shame on you for saying that. This is a breeze for me. I swear by my honor that I will talk to her on the phone. "

- A man offered a cigarette to another, and the latter refused to take it because he does not smoke. The first man said to him, "Shame on you if you refused my gift!" The second had to take it and smoke it.

Despite the simplicity of this situation that we often see in our daily lives; it unmistakably demonstrates the clear conflict between the meaning of shame and its use.

After presenting the aforementioned situations, the question remains: Does the definition of shame align with the previous situations in which it was used?

Meaning, if the definition of shame means refraining from wrong behaviors that don't please the society, conflict with the values and standards, and stress on the right behavioral values and standards; then what are the values and standards that the concept of shame seeks to preserve and consolidate? Are these the values of cheating, disregarding rights, promoting smoking, and seducing a woman? Have the criteria for judging things and evaluating others become based on concepts of favoritism, nepotism, and personal connections? Have moral principles declined and been replaced by personal interests? Have the standards that used to punish wrongdoers and reward those who do right, regardless of special considerations, disappeared? Have they been replaced by standards based on favoritism, which hinder the implementation of principles and work rules? Have the rules of "doing favors" become the new norm, eroding the formality and transforming it into informality, like mites eating away at the body of what used to be formal?

The following section is connected to the previous discussion. Therefore, if there is a discrepancy in the understanding of shame and its application in everyday life, it is natural to expect conflicts and disagreements regarding cultural values and standards, as well as a perception of shame that may be perceived as having double standards.

II- Shame and the duality of perception:

When I refer to the duality of perception, I am pointing to the disagreement over the definition of behavioral norms. If the term "shame" encompasses all actions that go against societal values and standards, then there should be consistent criteria for evaluating such actions. However, in certain everyday situations, it becomes apparent that each person views shame from their own perspective, which may contradict the perspectives of others. It is as if there are no fixed or specific rules and standards, as everyone perceives shame through their own unique lens, resulting in varying shapes and forms of shame. Let's examine some everyday situations to understand the dual nature of our perception of shame and how the concept of shame is influenced by the diversity of perceptions and cultural values associated with it.

- A girl criticized her mother for arriving home late, remarking, "You know, mom, it's not appropriate for you to come home so late. What would the neighbors say about us?" The mother retorted, "If you truly understood the concept of shame, you would have realized that it's inappropriate for you to interrogate and question your mother in this manner. Who should be the one to give advice among us?"

If we look closely at this short situation, it will become clear to us that in these two different situations, shame was used to support two different perceptions of it. The first situation is where the girl who identified the mistake in her mother's behavior, which is her late return to home. So the daughter decided to address the issue with her mother and bring it to her attention for future consideration, knowing how harshly a woman can be judged for returning home late. The daughter wanted to alert her mother to this behavior in order to jointly preserve their reputation. As for the second situation, the mother completely refused to discuss her wrong action with her daughter. Instead, she launched into what I call a "marginal" argument that was not originally the subject of discussion, about who has the right to question and hold the other accountable. It was as if the whole situation revolved around the status of power and who enforcers it in the household, and not about the mother's wrong practice. Also, the mother didn't miss the opportunity to support her argument by using shame, as the girl did, in order to project it in the behavior of the other.

- A man says to his niece who came home late, "It is a shame for a girl like you to be out this late. Would you like it when people say you are not good girl." The mother replied, "It would be a shame if you allowed someone to say so about my daughter, because whoever and whatever disgraces her disgraces you."

- A woman gossips and slanders another woman in the presence of their neighbor. Then the neighbor said what she heard to this other woman. After being confronted, the first woman admonished her neighbor, saying, "Isn't it a shame that I would tell you something, and you go and spread it?" The neighbor replied, "Isn't gossip shameful? Actually, it's a shame for you to slander someone who is absent."

- In a family discussion about whether to hold a wedding ceremony for a family member shortly after the recent death of a relative, one family member expressed, "I think it would be shameful. We should postpone the wedding for at least forty days. What would people say about us?" Another relative disagreed, saying, "Brother, I believe the sooner the better. It's shameful that we let other people dictate our actions. After all, these are our family events, not theirs. Haven't you heard the saying, 'A girl can get married at her father's funeral'?"

- A man saw a woman on the street wearing short and tight clothes, so he looked at her disapprovingly and criticized her, saying, "Shame on the one who let you leave your house in this way." She replied, "Shame on you for looking at me. You are supposed to lower your eyes and mind your business."

- In a discussion about teaching sex education in schools, one man objected, saying, "By God, it's shameful to witness what's happening here! What kind of sex education are you going to teach the children? Are we going to be like America!? Instead of studying their school books, they'll be flipping through inappropriate magazines." Another man responded, disagreeing, "What's shameful about our children learning about this from qualified specialists? It's better than them learning about it from their friends or satellite channels."

- A TV program on a satellite channel was showing cases of customary marriages in our society. One man disapproved of such a discussion, telling his friend, "Lord, what a shame to tarnish the image and reputation of our country and our daughters by publicizing such issues in this way." His friend replied, opposing, "Why do you consider it shameful? What's shameful is committing this act and not speaking publicly about it. The phenomenon actually exists, so why should we bury our heads in the sand like ostriches?"

- An elderly man on a bus says to a young man, "What a shame! Come on, son, I'm an old man, let me sit down in your place." The young man replied, "What shame are you speaking of, uncle? Do you think that I'm a small kid? Find some other kid and tell him to let set down in his place."

-          A group of rural women criticizing a man who's making his wife walk in front of him, as he believes that women are supposed to walk in front of men. In the meanwhile, they think this behavior is shameful; "it is shameful for a man to walk behind a woman."

-          A young child calls his older cousin by his name, without titles. The cousin tells him, "Shame on you, son for call me by my name like that! I'm not that young to play with you." The father of the child, and the uncle of the man speaking, replies telling his son, "Call him by his name and do not care about him. You are equal to him."

The previous situations revealed the duality of our perception of shame, and the conflict over the standards that constitute it. For more clarification about what shame is and what form it takes, the next section will revolve around this subject.

III- Shame: Moral flaws vs. physical flaws:

The proposed definition of shame is "deviating from (going against) what society deems correct with regard to values, traditions, and behavioral standards." This requires a deliberate intention on the part of the actor to deviate from societal norms. When such deviation occurs, the actor's behavior becomes a subject of shame, admonishment, and criticism. Accordingly, anything that goes against the values, norms, and moral standards of society is considered shameful or flawed. This meaning becomes evident when we analyze everyday situations, where the behavior that is socially judged as "shameful" is often manifested through actions that deviate from what is accepted by society. To clarify this, I will refer to some topics of moral flaws that are related to deviating from (going against) the ethical standards, which include:

-          Young men flirting with girls in the street.
-          Girls dancing at wedding ceremonies.
-          Swearing, cursing and using profanity in public places.
-          Disrespect of the elderly.
-          Inconsiderateness of others.

- Disclosure of secrets.
- Wearing revealing clothing.
- Disobedience of a wife to her husband.

And many other moral flaws by which a person goes against the society's standards and norms. So what about the person who does not engage in such behavior? According to this concept, he would be doing the right thing and succeeded in avoiding any act that might lead him to be shamed. However, this person may face social stigma due to physical attributes that do not conform to societal norms and values. These characteristics may be beyond the individual's control, yet society perceives them as flaws. For instance:

- Being too short or too tall.
- Obesity and skinniness.
- Disability.
- Dark skin color.
- Infertility.
- Curly/kinky hair.

The society not only highlights inherent flaws in individuals, but also labels them with sarcastic and mocking terms. For example:

- A thin woman: "She so skinny like she's coming from a famine."
- A short man: "A midget who is so close to the ground."
- A man with a gentle or soft voice is labeled as "effeminate."
- A dark-skinned woman: "An enslave girl."
- Curly/kinky hair: "Like steel wool."
- A barren woman: "like a wasteland."

IV- Shame: Wrongness vs. Sin:

When reflecting on the usage of the word "shame" in everyday situations, I have noticed that there are no standard degrees by which we can define behaviors as shameful. When we judge a behavior, we do not rely on a specific standard by which we describe one behavior as shameful and the other as not that shameful. Rather, we notice that shame fluctuates between concepts of wrongness and sin, in terms of both form and content, to the point that it is often difficult to differentiate between the two patterns. When discussing wrongness and sin, I do not mean to make value judgments or moral evaluations of individuals' practices. As a researcher, that is not my role. Rather, my intention is to highlight that there is no fixed standard for gauging what is considered shameful in relation to individuals' behaviors. To clarify this, a comparison was made between two different types of practices to highlight the gap and contrast between them in terms of degree. One practice may be simple while the other crude, yet both are considered shameful. And we label them as (shame/shameful).

Everyday life is replete with contradictions and diverse practices when it comes to the use of shame. In this context, I will draw a comparison between two situations where shame can range from being seen as wrongful to sinful, or differ in terms of form and content.

- A group of women, with a girl among them, were telling sexual jokes. Once the girl shared a joke like them, one of the women quickly said to her sharply, "No! It's shameful for a girl like you to talk about sex." (The lady said the sentence very firmly to the girl.)

A woman who has a sexual relationship with a man who's not her husband. She told her friend about him and the friend advised her by saying, "You must end this relationship. Shame on you for cheating on your husband and yourself more than that. Then again, you must take your children into account."

The common factor between these two situations is (sex), but the difference between them comes from the fact that the first situation is just about telling sexual jokes, while the second is an illegal sexual practice. The two situations are not completely equal in degree, yet the word (shame/shameful) was used in both of them.

Let's take another look at two other situations about women's pregnancy:

-        An older married woman, aged over fifty, discovered that she was pregnant, which led to her children becoming angry and quarreling with her. Her eldest daughter chastised her, saying, "It's disgraceful for you, Mom, to be pregnant at your age. What would I say to my friends at the university? Mom is still young and pregnant? What would people say about us? You should get rid of this fetus."

-        An unmarried woman has an affair with a man and found out that she is pregnant from him. She tells him, "This is a disaster. What a great shame! I can't confront anyone about it. What would people say when they know that I'm not married? I must abort it."

The use of the word (shame/shameful) in the two situations did not differentiate between pregnancy at an inappropriate age, as in the first situation, and adulterous pregnancy, as in the second situation.

Likewise in this third couple of situations:

- A man saw a colleague of his shaking hands with a female colleague of theirs, and he admonishes him about the prohibition of shaking hands with women, saying: "It is a shame to shake hands with her. You could just greet her."

- A man admonishes a friend of his who is involved in a sexual relationship with a woman, telling him, "Shame on you, brother! Look at your wife! you are married to a perfect woman."

The use of the word "shame/shameful" in the previous two situations does not recognize the difference between greeting by shaking hands and an illicit relationship, as both are shameful.

Finally, in the fourth couple of situations, shame fluctuates between wrongness and sin:

- A young man crosses his legs as his father approaches. His mother scolds him, saying, 'What a shame! When your father enters the room, you should uncross your legs.'"

- A young man attacked his father and insulted him. So the father retorts, saying to him, "Shame on you for cursing me! I'm your father. You really are ill-mannered."

There is no doubt that these two situations demonstrate a wrongful act that both young men committed, even if they vary in degree. While the mother found, in the first situation, that her son did not respect his father enough when he crossed his legs in his father's presence, in the second situation, the young man has actually cursed his father. And the two situations in which the word "shame/shameful" was used, despite the apparent discrepancy between them.

Thus, the previous situations reveal that the use of the word "shame/shameful" does not make much difference regarding practices that can be overlooked and those that are unanimously considered disgraceful.

V- Shame: Prohibiting vs. Allowing:

The title may suggest that shame is utilized to prohibit practices that go against societal values, while allowing those that align with them and are not deemed problematic by society. However, this meaning did not occur to me while writing this title. Rather, my intention was to highlight that the same practice can be condemned using shame in one context, while in another context it may be allowed and even approved of without being considered shameful, even though it is the same practice in both cases. Everyday situations reveal this clearly, as we see fluctuations in the use of shame to either prohibit or allow certain practices. However, it can be unclear when a practice is prohibited or allowed. This is what the following situations will reveal:

In a discussion between two men about helping their wives at home, One person said to another, "I would help my wife with anything at home. But when a guest comes, she will not expect me to help her with anything in front of him. She will do everything by my command. Do you think I want the guest to think that I don't know how to run the house?" The other person responded in agreement, saying, "You're right. I do everything at home, even the laundry, but she's the one who hangs it out. It's shameful for a man to stand on the balcony and hang out the laundry."

The practice here is the same: helping their wives with household chores. As we can see, the two men did not consider it shameful to help their wives, as they explicitly expressed their agreement with each other. However, they deemed it absolutely shameful to be seen doing household chores in public. Thus, they prohibited in public what they allowed in secret and considered it shameful.

- A girl's family forbade her from wearing makeup, even when she was going to university. Her mother would express her disapproval by saying, "It's shameful. What kind of impression are you trying to make with that red and green makeup? Do you want people to think you're going to a nightclub?" However, when a groom came to propose to the girl, whom the family had approved of, she decided to meet him without any makeup on her face. However, her mother stopped her and scolded her, "Wait a second! You're going to meet the groom like this, without makeup? Just washing your face?! Put on some red lipstick. Or do you want people to think you're not into this marriage or something?"

This situation highlights the inconsistency between the concepts of nurturing and guardianship. The same behavior may be allowed in one context but prohibited in another due to inconsistent rules.

- A mother permits her daughter to wear makeup when going out and attending university, but only when the father is out of town for work. However, in his presence, the girl cannot put on makeup, because the father considers that not only shameful, but a crime that deserves punishment.

The earlier situation demonstrates that the decision to permit or prohibit a practice is based on the severity of the resulting punishment. In this instance, the girl refrains from wearing makeup in her father's presence due to fear of his assault, but feels comfortable applying it when he is absent.

- A mother prohibits her children from doing certain behaviors in the presence of guests, such as speaking loudly, interrupting the guest when speaking, and making trouble and noise. In the meantime, these behaviors are allowed to the children all the time at home in the absence of strangers.

- When a woman visits her village, she faces criticism from the villagers for wearing trousers. They shame her by saying, 'How dare you wear trousers! What will the men wear then?" So she stopped wearing them when she went to her village, and only wore them while being in the city.

If the use of shame can prohibit and allow the same practice at the same time in different contexts, are there specific individuals who are targeted with the word 'shameful' to refrain from certain practices? Despite the fact that these practices are allowed for other people? This is what the following situations will reveal:

- A young man flirted with a girl who is his relative. And when a relative admonished the young man's father for his son's behavior, the father said to his son, "Couldn't you find another girl to flirt with other than your relative? There are plenty of fish in the sea. Just flirt with anyone you want, except for your relative. What a shame, indeed!"

The practice in question is flirting, which is deemed inappropriate. If this behavior is considered wrong, then it should be deemed wrong in all cases, whether the person being flirted with is a relative or not. However, we see that the father in the previous situation prohibited his son from flirting with a relative and has allowed this act and accepted it with other women with whom his son is not related.

- In a conversation between two men about marital infidelity, one of them said, "When a man cheats on his wife, He is definitely wrong, no doubt. But his wife is supposed to forgive him so that their lives can go on. It's just a fling that will end soon, and he will return to her. So she must forgive him. As for the woman, if she was the one who cheated on her husband, then this is another case. A cheating woman does not deserve to live. Her husband will not be a man if he forgives her." His friend replied, "You are right."

- A group of men were having a private meeting where they discussed their intimate relations with their wives. They shared details of these relationships but avoided mentioning their wives' names. Instead, they referred to them simply as 'the wife,' as they all considered it shameful to mention their wives' names.

The friends prohibited mentioning their wives' names and allowed themselves to share the finest details of their intimate relationship.

- Two men were sitting alone by themselves; one of them told a sexual joke, and they laughed loudly. Their laughs drew the attention of their wives, so they entered the room quickly to ask about the reason for their laughter. So they kept silent, as the one who told the joke was ashamed of his friend's wife and said to his wife, "It's shameful to tell when the other woman is sitting here.

I cannot say anything now." After the two wives insisted, he told the joke to his wife in a low voice, and then the wife told it to her friend in private.

As if what's shameful is not the content of the joke but rather to whom it's said. The joke was allowed for men separately as well as for women separately, but it was totally prohibited when they were all together.

- A mother curses her child whenever he commits an unacceptable act. In one instance, the mother cursed at her child, and the child cursed back at her with the same words she had used. The mother scolded him harshly, saying, "Boy! Shame on you for saying that. Do not curse at me ever again! How could someone curse at their own mother? I can curse you, but you can't."

- A mother rebuked her daughter when her male university classmate called her at home, saying, "It's a shame to let a stranger call you at home." On the other hand, the mother does not think there's anything wrong with her son's female university classmates calling him, saying, "He is a man. There is nothing he would be ashamed of. However, girls are accountable for each and every action."

- A mother discovered her two daughters, aged ten and eight, playing in the street. She scolded the older one, saying 'Shame on you!' while leaving the younger one unscathed. When the eldest daughter asked her, "Why didn't you beat my sister too?" The mother said, "She is young and does not understand anything, but you are old. You should know right from wrong."

- At a village school, a group of male and female teachers engaged in a discussion about a female supervisor who comes from the city for inspections. The supervisor, a widow, wears trousers, and they mockingly nicknamed her 'the trouser teacher.' Once she leaves, the teachers proceed to crudely mock and ridicule her, with one of them remarking, "This woman has no respect for her age. I don't know why she acts this way?" Another one replied, "If she had a man who controls her, she wouldn't do so." While a third teacher said, "Don't they say that she is a widow? Maybe she's looking for a man and she wants to get married." A female teacher replied to them, "Shame on you all for saying this. The woman is minding her own business, and it is clear that she is polite and respectful," one of the male teachers replied, "It's a shame if we're talking about some respectable woman." But this one deserves what people say about her because she's the one who is degrading herself."

Thus, the use of shame fluctuates between prohibiting and allowing. Gossip is a shameful act, but its practice depends on the nature of the person against whom it is slandered, and not because it is a prohibited behavior. Therefore, we see gossip is prohibited against respectable women and allowed against the disrespectful ones. But who has the right to judge whether a person is respectable or not? Is this limited to women alone, without men?

- An employee at the real estate registry uses the word 'shame' when the crowd is pushing and going ahead of their turn in line in front of him, saying, 'Shame on you, people! There is a line that you should respect." On the other hand, he allows chaos, disorder, and non-compliance for a beautiful woman or a man in a suit who appears to be of high social status.

It was clear from the above who can allow the practice of shaming and who can prohibit it. We have seen in these situations what is allowed for men and prohibited for women, what is allowed for adults but not for children, and what is allowed for women but not for girls.

VI- Shame between incitement and warning:

The effectiveness of using shame as a tool to incite or warn against certain behaviors depends on how it is articulated and directed. The usage of the word 'shame/shameful' can either achieve the intended goal of preventing and warning against wrong behavior, or it may weaken the concept and even be used to incite such behavior. In this context, I am reminded of a classic scene from Egyptian cinema where the master of the household makes advances towards the maid, and she tries to resist by using her famous catchphrase, 'This is a shame, sir! Someone might see us.' However, her words come out weak and hesitant, reflecting her awareness of her lower social status. Rather than discouraging him, her words are closer to approval and acceptance, rather than rejection and reluctance. Thus, the word 'shame' actually incites the action in this case.

There are many examples of the uses of shame that incite behaviors, which I drew from everyday situations, including:

A father was happy with his recently-speaking four-year-old son. He began urging the young boy to insult his older sister by saying, 'You're a donkey.' When the son repeated the same word or something similar to his father, the father laughed, saying, 'Shame on you, son! I'm your father, son of..." And he continues to laugh.

The way the father used the word 'shame' in the previous situation, and the happiness apparent on his face when uttering it, implicitly incited the son to continue the action and insult the father.

- In a similar situation, a little girl, no more than five years old, wears her mother's clothes, or puts on some of her mother's makeup or surprise her family by asking a naive sexual question. The mother says, laughing, 'This is shameful, my love! You can do this when you grow up.'"

A worker in one of the shops carried some items to the buyer at the door of his car, so when the buyer was about to give him some tips in exchange for his service, the worker smiled, looked down, and said, "That's a shame, sir. This is so kind of you. It's the least I can do for you."

The previous performances in earlier situations contained intentions that incited the behavior. The use of the word 'shame' in a low, neutral voice, combined with smiling or laughing facial features, collectively incites the recipient to take action.

This performance of the word 'shame' differs radically from another performance in which the word is used to 'warn' of certain behaviors that the person deems to be inappropriate, and that he/she should abstain from." The warning may take a silent form or performance, such as an eye look that a mother might direct at her son, to prohibit and warn him against engaging in inappropriate behaviors. In other cases, the word 'shame/shameful' may be used with expressions like 'What a shame!' or 'Shame on you!' accompanied by bulgy eyes, a fixed look, and a raised index finger pointed towards a person, in addition to a hoarse and strong voice when articulating the word. This tone of voice acts like a whip, lashing at consciences, breaking the will, and instilling a sense of shame and terror in the recipient, discouraging them from continuing the action. For example:

- A child was messing with his mother's handbag and tore up some of her papers. As soon as the mother saw him, she angrily said, 'Shame on you, boy!' Don't ever do that again, okay? You're going to be in big trouble if I catch you doing it once more."

To avoid repetition, many examples of using shame to warn of wrong behaviors will be cited in the next section in order to clarify the purpose behind the use of shame.

VII- Shame: Command vs. Prohibition:

In light of the aforementioned sections, in this chapter, I've addressed the various uses of shame. It may be appropriate now to ask about the function of shame (shaming) and the purpose behind its use. And when reading the everyday situations, in light of the proposed definition; the function of shame can be identified, which is commanding what society deems correct or what is socially accepted, and prohibiting what is wrong and contradicts the society's values and customs.

In everyday situations, it becomes apparent to the reader that shame is not solely used to command what is right and prohibit what is wrong. Many other methods of commanding and prohibiting exist in daily life. As a result, shame has been given other functions and purposes. And these functions can be defined in three forms, namely:

1) Suppression and denunciation
2) Coalition and dissension
3) Setting and losing boundaries.

1) Shame: Suppression vs. Denunciation

The use of shame (shaming) can contribute to suppressing and restricting behaviors. When this word is used frequently, restraints and prohibitions increase in a man's life. Thus, shame becomes a tool for suppressing behaviors. There are many examples of suppressing behaviors, including:

- A school principal discovered an autograph book in which some female students had exchanged written mementos. Although the mementos didn't contain anything incriminating, the principal rebuked and scolded the owner of the book, saying, "It's a great shame for you to bring something like this to school. I'm warning you - this is the last time I'll allow you to have something like this with you again."

- A husband and wife were at the entrance of their house when the husband saw a cat on the stairs. He grabbed the cat and scared his wife with it as a joke, but she was terrified and screamed loudly. The husband then reprimanded her harshly, saying, "Shame on you! You shouldn't raise your voice like that. What would people say?"

- A mother was talking to her son, giving him some warnings, "Today we will have guests. Don't act naughty. Don't say a bad word. And don't get your clothes dirty. It is a shame if you do so."

- A in a conversation between a brother and his divorced sister who insisted on living alone, he told her, "A divorced woman is closely held accountable for her actions. You must know that now you are not the same as before. Without a doubt, it's shameful that you live on your own. Also, you cannot go out as much as you want."

Thus, the use of shame turned into a means to suppress and restrict behaviors, through commands and prohibitions. What harm is it for the school principal if some student has an autograph, in which she exchanged some written mementos with her classmates, to the point that he prohibit the student from bring it again? Why does this husband care more about what others might think of him because of his wife's terrified reaction to his bizarre prank, rather than the fact that his prank caused her to feel scared in the first place? Instead of taking responsibility for his actions, he commanded her to stop screaming. Why did the mother give so many prohibitions to her son just because they were having guests over? All these commands and prohibitions only indicate the extent of cultural values and traditions in which the word "shame" is used to suppress and restrict behaviors.

However, shame isn't used only to suppress behaviors; it's also used to denounce them. There are many examples of denunciation that we practice against each other in everyday life, including:

- A man who's over seventy years old and wearing a red shirt was told by another man, "Shame on you, man! You must respect your age. Your actions should reflect your age."

- A man in his sixties, with gray hair, was standing on the street catcalling girls and women. One woman confronted him, saying, "Shame on you, old man! You're acting so bizarrely!"

It's like the society sees that committing foolish acts is only for young people, and that young people have their recklessness and foolishness, while those who are older must do what is right and stay away from childish behavior.

- A woman criticizes another woman in the street who wears very short and tight clothes, telling her, "The shame is not on you, but on your husband who allowed this."

- A man went to visit a young man in his house with whom he had previous association. When the young host proposed to marry the daughter of this man and asked his opinion, the man replied, "Shame on you, man! Your father had much grace and docurm. Come to my house and propose to my daughter there. Only then I will tell you my opinion. Or what do you think?"

- A father says to his child who kept crying because his mother was away at work, "Shame on you, son, for crying like girls."

- In a feud between two families to settle their disputes, in the presence of a number of men and two women, one from each family, the first woman stood up and gave her opinion on this dispute. Before she could finish her talk, the other woman interrupted her, saying: "You let you men sit aside silently and let your women speak. I swear, in our family, women value their men. It's shameful for a woman to speak while her husband is sitting by her."

- A man cursed and insulted his wife, so she complained about him to her family. When they came to her marital home to find out the cause of their dispute, the husband said, "She is a neglectful woman at home and wastes all her time in her workplace." Her uncle said to him, "You accept her contributions to the household expenses, don't you? Isn't it shameful that you need your wife's money instead of giving her financial support? Instead, you yell at her and insult her. Isn't it shameful for a decent man like you to say such things to his wife? What have you left for the scoundrels?"

-       A mother scolds her daughter, who got into a heated argument with her, "That's not your fault. Shame on me for not raising you properly and teaching you how to talk to your mother!"

These examples demonstrates what I concluded; that denunciation is used to taunt someone we believe to be wrong, condemn his action, and rebuke him for ding such action.

2) Shame: Coalition vs. Dissension:

Shame is used to foster cohesion among people and to encourage maintaining good relations with family, neighbors and friends. People should cooperate with each other, and people have rights over their families. If we contemplated everyday life, we will find that shame is present factor in fostering harmony among people. For example:

- A neighbor admonishes his neighbor for not asking about him, saying, "Isn't it a shame that we live next door, yet you don't knock on it and ask about me? Don't you remember, brother, that the Prophet commended us to have good relations with our neighbors?"

- A child and his cousin were fighting over a toy. The uncle came and took the toy and gave it to his son. So his brother said to him, "Isn't it a shame to create a divide between my son and yours? They're like brothers, playing together as children. My son is just as important as yours."

- A father admonishes his son on the phone, saying, "Shame on you son! You forgot your father and mother who raised you and let life distract you. We also have a right over you."

- A mother urges her son to visit his sick neighbor, saying, "What a shame, my son! You should go and visit your neighbor. People should be there for each other."

- A mother was making sure that a teacher is taking care of her son, saying, "I won't pressure you into taking care of him, Professor!" He said to her, "That would be a shame, madam. He is like my son. Rest assured."

- A father was urging his son, "Don't forget to serve the people of your country. That would be a shame, son! They are your family and your people. Only a vile man turns a blind eye to his origin."

However, shame continues its usual fluctuation between the two extremes. For instance, it fluctuates between wrongness and sin, and between prohibiting and allowing at another time, as well as between inciting and warning at a third time. Here, it fluctuates again between coalition and dissension; as it aims at fostering coalition among the society's members and urging them to find harmony and establish brotherhood. Rather, we find it asserts dissension among people. People are of different statuses and they are not equal; rich and poor, respected and disrespected, men and women, or young and old. This will also be demonstrated in the following situations:

- A group of veiled girls were criticizing other non-veiled girls, for their appearance and clothes, saying, "What are they doing to themselves? What are they wearing? Isn't it a shame? This is not how we dress."

- A father of a rural girl rebuked her, saying, "Shame on you for imitating your cousin and dressing like her! You don't get to act like her. She lives in Cairo. We have no business with Cairo's girls. We have our own customs and traditions."

- In a conversation between businessmen, one of them, who works abroad, said, "Whenever I need Egyptian labor to travel with me, I prefer to take them from the countryside. Because those from the countryside know what's shameful and respect the moral code, unlike those from the urban cities."

- A mother forbids her daughter from befriending a liberal girl, telling her, "Shame on you my child for being around her! Her ethics are totally different from ours. She has no shame. You must cut her off."

In a conversation between two teachers from two different towns, the first teacher denounced his colleague's town where all its resident merchants and wives sell alongside each other in the markets. On the other hand, the other town of the first teacher took pride in its people who are poor, yet their wives do not go out with them to sell in the markets. As he said, "Don't you think it's a shame for a woman to work outside the home?"

- A group of men were talking about helping their wives in the household chores. One of them said that he would help his wife to the minimum possible. And another one said that he goes out to bring the household needs to his wife. A third one commented, saying, "It's a shame for a man to cook and do the laundry. A man's a man and a woman's a woman."

- A father says to his young son, "Shame on you for crying like a woman! You're a man, and men don't cry. What did you left for spoilt little girls?"

- A mother says to her son when she found out that he was playing with his friends in the street, "Shame on you, boy! get out of the street and come at once. What are the difference between you now and the street kids?"

- A car owner was talking to a mechanic who was repairing his car, saying, "I hope that the car doesn't break down again, or find problems with it once I drive it." The mechanic replied to him: "That would be a shame, sir! I am not a rookie."

- A woman confided to her friend a topic, and after she finished talking, she said to her, "Don't tell anyone about this." Her friend said to her, "That would be a shame! I'm not a little girl!"

- A woman who is a member of an elite club refused to allow a kid to enter the toilet inside the club because he is wearing a T-shirt of another lower-class popular club. She prevented him and summoned security, telling them, "He's not a member. He could be carrying microbes. It's really shameful to witness what's happening here. How could you let someone who does not have a membership card enter the club?"

Then what happen when shame consolidates differentiation among people and classifies them into young and old, men and women, and rich and poor? This is the subject of the next section.

3) Shame: setting boundaries and losing them:

Once shame classified people into two groups; the first part is similar to be familiar with themselves, and the other is different to criticize, reject and differ from the other part. So, it's natural that shame sets boundaries among these people, which define the nature of the relationship between them where it becomes a shame for them to cross it. Upon reflecting on the everyday situations, we found that that life is full of situations in which shame draws red lines; to set boundaries in the relations between people so that they don't cross them. For example:

- In a conversation between employees and a colleague of theirs who insulted the manager, their colleague told them, "Didn't you see how he spoke to me and what did he say to me? Of course I had to curse at him." They said to him, "That's shameful! He's still your boss and he has power over you. You should have made some compromise."

- In a conversation between two relatives with an age gap of more than fifteen years, the younger one addressed the older relative by their name without using any titles. The older relative rebuked them, saying "It's shameful for you to call me by my name like that. I'm not a child, so please take me seriously."

- A father kicked his son out of the house for being late at night. The mother said to the father, "It is a shame that you expel him from the house, Hajj." He said to her: "Are you are telling me that it is a shame? Are you the one who is going to teach me about shame? Did you forget who you are or something?"

- In a conversation between two employees, after one of them was promoted to became a boss over the other, his subordinate colleague was joking with him as usual. The boss said to him, "Shame on you for forgetting who you are while talking to me! Be careful from now on!"

- A middle-aged man was getting out of his luxury car, when a doorman said to him, "You can't park here," to which the man replied angrily, "Shame on you for talking to me like that. Don't you know who I am?"

- A high school student disagreed with his teacher's opinion. The teacher said to him, "Shame on you son for arguing with your teacher in this way. There are boundaries that you must not cross."

- During a conversation with his female co-worker, an employee delved into some of her personal matters. In response, she firmly stated, "Sham on you, sir. There are boundaries that should be respected when we speak to each other. Please be mindful of that."

Just as shame is used to set boundaries and create red lines between people, it can also, in some cases, erase the very boundaries it was meant to establish. There are situations where these boundaries disappear and are lost, such as:

- In a conversation between two relatives, one of whom is at least ten years younger than the other. The young man addressed the older one by the title "Sir". Therefore, the older man said to him, "Sir? what a shame! we don't have to be this formal. We are like brothers."

- A woman calls another (aunt) due to the age gap between them. Therefore, the older woman said to her: "Aunt? Do you think that I'm an elderly woman or something like that? Shame on you! Do you think I gave birth to someone your age? Or do you think you're still a little baby?"

- A man was thanking a friend of his for standing by his family when he was traveling. His friend said to him, "It's a shame that you're thanking me. I didn't do anything other than my duty. Why are you making a big deal of it? If you thank me, it may make me feel like I owe you something, and I don't want that to come between us."

- A manager was talking to an employee and addressed her by "kiddo" and he continued, saying, "Are you upset with I say "kiddo" to you?" And she told him, "That would be a shame, boss! I know what it means. You cherish and consider me like your daughter, because you call me like your daughters."

As I reflect on previous everyday situations and the role of shame in shaping social interactions, I am struck by its powerful impact on individuals. It can enable certain behaviors while restricting others, repress undesired actions, and create divisions and boundaries among people. Ultimately, it reinforces social hierarchies and reinforces social differentiation by elevating some and marginalizing others.

So, by whom is this power represented? Does it have delegates? And what are their mechanisms for consolidating it?

The following pages will be an endeavor to try to answer these questions.

3

How is the Strong Self Shaped in the Arab Culture?

I- Forms of Power in Everyday Life

When contemplating the forms of power in everyday situations, I found them multiple and diverse. However, I believe that they can be summed up in two main forms, which are:

1. Gender relations.

2. Age relations.

1) Power in Gender Relations: The implications of the masculine culture

Representations and forms of masculinity in everyday situations are linked to societal concepts related to masculinity, and the related cultural indicators that determine the nature of the relations among the society members, such as the relation between men and women, for example. Hence, the masculine culture in society represents a power that's present in the practices of individuals. Perhaps the most powerful manifestation of this culture is that it does not need to justify its presence in the society. According to Bourdieu, the masculinity-centered view imposes itself as a lived reality and does not need to be expressed in discourses seeking to give it legitimacy. (Pierre Bourdieu, 2001, p. 22). This can be seen clearly in the masculinity representations in everyday life. Hence, reading the representations of power in everyday life in isolation from the prevailing masculine culture is a misguided effort.

Perhaps one of the most common representations of power is the power that men exert over women. However, this is not the only representation, but there is also the power exercised by men over men, women over women, and women over men. The tools used by those who exercise power are often rooted in masculine cultural norms that are so deeply ingrained that they become normalized behavior.

Daily life is deeply influenced by the implications of masculine culture, which can be distilled into four distinct power dynamics: men's power over women, men's power over other men, women's power over other women, and women's power over men. To better understand these representations, let's explore a few examples:

The power of men over women:

As previously mentioned, the representations of masculinity are deeply rooted in the dominant masculine culture within society. This culture introduces ideas that establish masculinity as the source of strength, toughness, and rationality in society, while femininity is portrayed as weak, fragile, lazy, and mentally deficient. As a result, this culture grants masculinity the exclusive right to control femininity completely, dictating its entire existence and directing its behavior in a manner that serves the interests of the culture. The power exercised by men over women is one of the most common representations of this meaning. The following situation can further explain this point:

- A husband made his wife, who is a teacher, swear on the Holy Quran that she would never drink tea in the school where she works. She agreed to this condition. However, when she became tired of adhering to this oath, she asked him, "Why did you forbid me from drinking tea at school? I work five classes per day. There are a lot of kids in the classes. At the end of the day, I can't even open my eyes because of the headache. So, I feel like I need a cup of tea. What is the reason for this prohibition?" Her husband replied, "Because I don't want you to talk to any of your male colleagues at work. I work and I know the ridiculous things that go around between men and women when they drink some tea together." The wife replied, "It's just tea! What's that got to do with these ridiculous things?" The husband said, "Drinking tea will provide a chance to talk until the tea is prepared. Then, you wait for it to cool down. And the chit-chat while drinking... So, do you understand now why I'm preventing you from drinking tea, madam?"

The following examples are given successively to illustrate the power men over women in everyday situations:

- A brother forbids his sister from going to university while she is applying makeup, saying, "I'm not allowing you to go to university looking like that." The girl replied, "All of my classmates go to university like this." The brother replied, "I don't wish my sister to leave the house like this. She might receive catcalls or suggestive glances from someone."

- A little brother prevents his older sister from laughing out loud while she is talking on the phone, telling her, "Shame on you! Lower your voice. People might hear you."

- A fiancé pressures his fiancée, who is excelling academically, to abandon her graduate studies and refuses to let her get a job at her college, insisting that "a woman should not attain a higher level of education than her husband."

- A newlywed husband hands his wife a list of commands she must adhere to, stating, "You need to understand that you have to ask for my permission before leaving the house. Visits to your family will be cut to the minimum. Before you befriend any women, I need to know them first. This way, I can determine who is appropriate for you to associate with and who is not. And if I reject one of them, that will be final and non-negotiable."

- A man forces his wife, a manager, to delete the contacts of her male colleagues from her mobile phone, telling her, "These contacts must be deleted immediately, or I will smash the phone on your head."

- A woman tells her sister over the phone that she is going out with her son and husband, mentioning the name of her son first then her husband's. Her husband rebuked her loudly, saying, "You are supposed to say my name first, madam! You should not favor your son over me."

These patterns illustrate how men exert power over women by socially assigned roles that allow them to correct and control women's behavior. These examples are not exhaustive, as there are other ways in which men exercise power over women. The following situations will demonstrate how men control women's bodies and restrict their movement to assert social control over them.

The following situations may express that:

- A husband prevents his wife from wearing bright colors while she is going to work, saying, "Why are you wearing such eye-catching outfit? It's not suitable for work." The wife replied, "What's wrong about it?" The husband replied, "Go and take off this ridiculous outfit and wear something decent."

- Another husband forces his wife to wear long, loose-fitting clothes, telling her, "I don't like my wife to get suggestive looks. You are expected to wear long and loose-fitting clothing that is not tight-fitting."

- A father violently hit his baby daughter on her legs after she fell from a seat in front of guests and her clothes rode up revealing her legs. He told her sharply, "Cover yourself, you shameless girl!"

The power of men over men:

Representations of masculinity do not stop at the power of men over women, but extend to include men over men as well. However, the power that men exercises over men differs in nature from the power that is exercised over a woman. With women, we have found that it's based on controlling women, directing their behavior and correcting it. As for men, it stems from the concepts of masculine culture, where men are seen differently than women. The following two examples may illustrate the difference:

- A young man reprimands his friend for refusing to have a relationship with a girl, and telling him, "You must live your age. You must love and be loved. Only girls are held accountable for their actions. But you are a man and there is nothing can shame you."

- A man admonishes his friend for accepting his wife's contribution to the household expenses, telling him, "Shame on you for being OK with your wife sharing your household expenses. Men are the caretakers of women. Today, your wife share the household expenses, and tomorrow she will go head to head with you."

As is evident in the two examples, the power exercised over men is fundamentally different from the power exercised over women. The reason for this difference can perhaps be attributed to the masculine culture that affords men the freedom to act as they please, as they are not subject to shame. In contrast, women are often deprived of their rights and subjected to numerous restrictions, preventing them from competing with men on an equal footing.

The power of women over women:

This is another manifestation of masculine culture, although this time the person exercising power is a woman. She exercises power over another woman like herself, embodying all the concepts of masculine culture that prioritize strictness, toughness, rigidity, and dominance, all in favor of men. The following situations may clearly illustrate this form:

-     A woman expresses her grievances to her mother regarding her husband's abusive behavior, citing frequent beatings and harsh treatment. The mother's response, however, is callous: "What's the problem? He is your husband and has authority over you. Listen to him, and don't make him mad or sad, and he will treat you well."

- A husband insisted that his wife should not visit her mother. And when she did not comply with her husband's command and was about to leave, her mother-in-law got on her way and told her harshly, "As long as your husband commands you not go out, then you don't get to go out. You must ask his permission first."

- A woman, who wear Niqab, advises her co-worker not to wear trousers, telling her, "By the way, you should think about wearing skirts instead of these trousers, because it is forbidden (Haram) and does not cover anything of your body. It also attract men. I personally forbade my daughter, who is in the 8th Grade, from wearing trousers at home in front of her young brother, in order to keep him chaste. And I don't care if she wasn't feeling comfortable at home."

Thus, the previous situations reveal that if woman who grew up embracing the masculine culture, she will absorb all masculine mentality very well. This can be seen clearly when men become the center of her life. She will be fully aware of her duties towards them, and get evaluated through her knowledge of him, or her loss of him. Hence, the woman's life get centered and molded to that, as she gives the man absolute sovereignty over her, and gives herself nothing but dependency on him. And if she deals with other women, she will treat them based on these concepts, while exercising power over them.

The power of women over men:

The previous patterns discussed the manifestations of masculine culture in the power dynamic between men and women, and between men themselves, as well as the power of women over other women. However, what about the power of women over men? This is what we will explore in the following lines, specifically how women exercise power over men.

Going through the situations, I can say that the traditional woman represents two pattern of exercising power over men. The first is the masculine pattern, and the second is the feminine pattern. In the first pattern, we observe a woman utilizing methods typically associated with men to exert her influence over them. As such, she appears as a strong, serious figure with sharp features and a commanding presence, often characterized by a loud voice, rigorous demeanor, and unwavering seriousness. She may even possess financial or physical strength to accomplish what is traditionally considered to be within the purview of men. Here are some of the situations that illustrate this:

- A woman is richer than her husband, and owns the marital home. She dictates her husband not to make a decision, even regarding the most delicate matters in his life, before referring to her, consulting her, and acting on her advice. She is the one who determines his friends, and the times of his going out and coming back home.

- A female manager deals with her male subordinates harshly and rigorously. And she uses her secret weapon, filing complaints against whoever confronts her, in addition to the successive investigations with them.

- A woman has a short temper, a loud voice, a strong build, and a sharp tongue. Her husband is too intimidated to intervene in their children's up-bringing, which she enforces with a cruel parenting style. He also does not dare to speak to any other woman so as not to provoke his wife's anger, otherwise she will hit him with a barrage of insults.

In the second pattern, the woman uses her beauty, vulnerability, tenderness, and the man's affection towards her to exert power over him. This is illustrated by the following two situations:

- A woman influences her husband with her tears, and her weakness to comply with her desires for going out, shopping, and doing entertainment activities.

- A woman uses her femininity and vulnerability to persuade her husband to allow her to keep her job, even though he initially ordered her to resign. She persists in her argument until she convinces him.

Through contemplating the two previous patterns of women's power over men, we find that they reveal the extent of traditional women's assimilation and absorption of masculine culture. The first pattern shows women using masculine traits to influence men through strictness, sharpness, and cruelty. However, they may not realize that by doing so, they are losing their own identity and assimilating with the dominant male, ultimately perpetuating the masculine culture. The same is true for the second pattern, where women use traits such as softness, weakness, beauty, tenderness, and flirting to manipulate men. This confines them within the societal framework created by masculine culture, perpetuating their subjugation.

2) The Power in Age-Related Relationships: Representations of the elders:

The forms of power that the elder person can take on are diverse and varied in daily life as the stronger party in a power relationship. These forms of power manifest in some of the following daily life situations:

- A father prevents his daughter from going out late with her friends.

- A father prohibits his daughter from dancing at a relative's wedding.

- A father rebukes his son for crying, telling him, "Shame on you for crying like girls. You're a man."

- A mother prohibits her son from playing in the presence of guests, telling him, "A good boy listens to what Mama says and does not act rude in front of strangers. That would be a shame. Do you want people to say that you were not raised well?"

- A mother scolds her son for playing in the street and getting his clothes dirty, telling him, "Shame on you for getting yourself dirty like those street kids. You should be ashamed of yourself. What would people think of you?"

- A mother instructs her daughters not to wear certain clothes that their father disapproves of, cautioning them, "Please avoid wearing those clothes. Your father has already expressed his dislike for them, and I don't want to provoke an argument. It would be better if you listened to him."

The body and the rules imposed on it are sources of conflict between parents and children. The more children want to be free, let loose, play, wear certain clothes, and give up wearing other clothes, the more parents try to exercise power over their children's bodies to control them. Here, the mother was setting certain disciplined behaviors for her young children in order to control their play time and body movement, especially in the presence of guests. In addition, we observe that she is the one who chooses clothes that both satisfy her husband's and society's standards, while also setting behavioral expectations that distinguish adolescence from childhood. The father also imposes restrictions on his children, prohibiting them from going out to play, wearing clothes that do not meet his approval, and even controlling their body movements, such as dancing and having fun.

However, the body is not the only domain in which the seniors impose their power on the juniors, as the following situations reveal some other behaviors that the seniors impose on the juniors:

- A father who is a dentist wants to impose his power over his son by pressuring him to enroll in the College of Dentistry so that he can eventually take over his father's clinic and clients. However, the son resists this pressure and instead opts to attend the Faculty of Engineering. The father tried to dissuade him from that, using temptation, saying, "If you attend the College of Dentistry, I will buy you a car with a chauffeur. I will make you the only student who goes to college with a chauffeur who opens the door to your car and carries your books. You will get to determine your pocket money. And after you graduate, the clinic is available, as are its clients." But the son refused and insisted on attending the Faculty of Engineering. Therefore, the father said, "You will get nothing from me, neither a car nor a chauffeur, if I insist on your opinion."

- A mother teaches her son certain behaviors by telling him, "You must knock on the door and ask permission before you enter. Also, when you go to a stranger, be careful not to convey our conversations to anyone else."

- A mother advises her son to consider a partner who values chastity, rather than a divorced woman. She believes that a young woman who has not been married before has more to lose and may hold different values.

The previous situations express the representation of the elder as the stronger party in the relationship. We find that the elder exercises power over someone who is younger than them, relying on the age factor, which is the main criterion for identifying the enforcer of power, or rather the elder. Based on this factor, the senior presents himself to the junior as the strongest, most knowledgeable, and wisest. Hence, according to the senior's vision, the junior could not do anything but obey him and carry out his orders even if they were against his will, regardless of this junior's age, knowledge or experience.

However, in everyday situations, it's revealed that the idea of the senior is not based solely on the age factor in order to exercise power over those who are younger. Rather, it is also based on other factors that have a significant impact on the behavior of others. This will be clarified in the following situations:

- A young employee in a company scolds a service worker, who is about sixty years old, for being late in doing a service for him, telling him, "You Shame on you; I'm asking you to do something, and you don't do it."

- A group of young men traveling between governorates on a bus asked for permission to make some purchases during a stop. However, they were late, and the conductor went looking for them. He found them smoking hookah in a cafe so he scolded them for delaying the journey. One of the young men interrupted him, sharply saying, "Please speak to us with respect. Don't you know from what families we are? Be respectful and be careful to secure your job."

- A woman is having difficulty obtaining the necessary official documents for her job due to the obstinacy of the employees in her workplace's administration. This has led her to bring her husband, who holds influence and power, to help her. As soon as the employees learned about his position, they rushed to complete the woman's papers as quickly as possible. And one of them commented, "It would be a shame if you sir asked for something and it wasn't provided."

- A head of a rural family exercises his authority over all members of his family and controls all aspects of their lives. He does not allow them to dispose of their properties without his permission and even dictates the names of their children. Any objection is met with the family's response, "It is shameful to dishonor the word of our family head."

- A rural woman gained influence among the women in her village and neighboring villages due to her husband's reputation as a healer who could cure them from witchcraft. Despite having no other notable achievements, she provided advice to the women about their personal affairs due to her status as the sheikh's wife.

In light of the aforementioned situations, it became clear that daily life produces other forms and standards of being senior other than the age factor, whose representatives succeed in influencing other, through such factors. As there are the head of a family, the head of a community, someone with great experience, someone with great wealth, and someone with a higher position. And other standards invented by those who are conflicting over the position of the head (senior) to win it and consolidate their power over those who are younger than them.

However, as we have seen the people in the previous patterns try to consolidate their power over those who are younger than them; is the juniors always subject to the power of the seniors? Or can juniors impose power over seniors as well? Is their imposition of such power necessarily considered a form of deviating from (going against) the traditions and prevailing culture in society? Or can they exercise power over the seniors based on the prevailing traditions and rules of shame, at the same time? So, how can juniors do that? And when is the moment when juniors can exercise power over seniors? Let us contemplate everyday life and the situations it contains that may have an answer to these questions:

- A woman quarrels with her neighbor in the street and curses her with the most horrible words. But her daughter came from the university and told her, "It is a shame to say this, Mum! That's not right. Please go inside. People are watching us."

- A widow came home late at night, and her daughter said to her, "You coming home very late, Mum! Why don't you take into account what people say?" The mother replied to her, "Are you judging me? Who is the mother among the two of us?" The daughter replied to her, "Of course I am your daughter, and you are my mother. But I do not want anyone to talk about us, and you must protect your reputation and mine as well."

- A teenager was watching his father smoking cigarettes, who always scolded and warned him against smoking and its harms. The teenager told him, "It's a shame, Dad! You give me an advice and you don't do it. Aren't these cigarettes harmful to health and a waste of money? So, why are you smoking now?"

- An old man is thinking of marrying a reckless young girl, and his son learned about it. So he said to him, "Is what I've heard true, Dad? This girl is not suitable for you. And she is also as young as your children. You must cut off her."

It is clear from the previous situations that juniors will not remain subject to the seniors' power all the time. Juniors can also exercise power over seniors, based on the power of custom and traditions at the moment when a seniors deviates from those cultural norms and traditions that he has always called for and imposed on those younger than him.

II: Traits of those who exercise power in everyday life:

This section is concerned with examining the traits and qualities that distinguish the power enforcer that makes him qualified to impose his will on others and direct them according to his desires and visions. Upon reflecting on the everyday situations, I can say that those who exercise power are characterized by a set of traits or qualities, the most important of which are:

1. Craving for power;

2. The tendency to act on behalf of others; and

3. Possessing knowledge.

1) Craving for power

One of the first traits of the power enforcer is an inherent trait in him that makes him always craving for power, possessing it in his hands, and imposing it on others. Let us contemplate the everyday situations to explore this trait:

- A father began to realize that his two teenage children (a boy and a girl) are getting bored with the heavy authority he's holding over them, as they were frequently reviewing his orders and being discontent when carrying them out. The father didn't want to change his approach towards them, nor did he want to confront them. Therefore, he informed them of his plans to implement democracy within the household. He would no longer impose his opinions on them, and any disagreement would be open to discussion and consultation until a mutually satisfactory solution is reached. All of this will be done through free voting. Then he distributed the votes among the members of the family. And in order to achieve democracy, he started with equality between the boy and the girl in the percentage of votes, by giving each of them one vote, then he gave the mother three votes, thus surpassing the total votes of her two children by one vote. So if the son and daughter agreed on an opinion that didn't please the mother, she would use her right and veto it. And the father gave himself six votes, surpassing the total of the family's votes by one vote. In this way, he gave the family democracy and kept for himself absolute authority over his house and the right to overthrow any opinion that went against his own.

This example clearly reveals the trait (craving for power) that characterizes the power enforcer. This father, who's the source of power and authority in the family, refuses to relinquish his authority over his two children, a refusal that was met with the conflict of his children with him, in addition to his refusal to sever his relationship with them. The solution the father found appeared to be democratic on the surface, but in reality, it was authoritarian and totalitarian. His aim was to make his two children accept his absolute authority willingly. Nevertheless, he didn't want to sever his relationship with them, which allowed him to stay aware of the finer details of their lives.

- A brother wanted to punish his little sister for opening his desk drawer and messing with his private papers. But the father forbade him by scolding him, "Are you going to hit her while I'm here?" His son replied, "She's the one who made a mistake, Dad. She messed with my papers." The father replied sharply, "You should come and complain to me and you can see what I'd do."

The father alone is the source of authority and power in the house. Therefore he alone has right of reward and punishment, and no one in the family can take away this right without his consent.

- A group of relatives were engrossed in a conversation about an important matter when one of them expressed his desire to buy a pack of cigarettes. He then called over one of the young men sitting nearby and instructed him, "Could you please quickly go and get me a pack of cigarettes?" The young man looked at him and said, "OK." Then he turned to his younger brother and said to him, "Go quickly and get your uncle a pack of cigarettes."

Undoubtedly, the uncle exerted his authority over the young man by using the imperatives "go" and "quickly," without considering that the young man's age may not allow such authority over him. The young man objected to this imposed authority by delegating the task to his younger brother, whom he could exercise authority over due to his age, using the same imperative verb "go."

- A frequently recurring scene in the downtown of the capital city is a street crowded with cars, where there are no policemen to control the traffic. A man takes it upon himself to control the traffic. He starts giving out instructions on what to do and what not to do, allowing some cars to pass and ordering others to stop and anyone who disobeys his orders is subjected to harsh scolding and reprimand.

The examples unfold, revealing that the "craving for power" is not related to a specific age, but rather it includes all ages. So we find young people imitating adults in this trait. And here are some examples:

A mechanic sent one of his underage assistant to buy some food, but the boy was a little late. And when he came back, the mechanic slapped him several times, saying, "Don't you ever go astray or distracted when I send on you to run some errands." The boy went to continue his work. But a customer saw him and asked him, "Tell me, what do you like to do when you grow up?" The boy said, "I'd like to be a mechanic." The client asked, "Why a mechanic?" The boy answered, "So that I can be like my boss and have power over everyone. And I can hit my young assistants."

- A little girl scolded her younger brother for getting ice cream all over his clothes, saying, "Look at you, you've stained your clothes. I'll tell mom to beat you."

- A little girl expressed her desire to become a doctor like her mother, so she can give injections to the bad kids, as she believed it would be a way to punish them.

A child dreams of becoming a teacher in the future. And when asked why, he said, "So that I could hit the kids."

These situations suggest that we all have a yearning for power and a strong desire to wield it, even when we may be tired of being subjected to it. We find ourselves drawn to the idea of exercising power over others, and if we have not had the chance to do so, we long for it even more, dream about it, and crave for it.

2) The tendency to act on behalf of others:

The second trait of the power enforcer is that not only does he give himself the right to interfere in the lives of others, but he also goes beyond that by making decisions on their behalf. There are several situations that can clearly illustrate this trait:

- A man has a brother who is one year younger than him, works in a prestigious position and is not married. A friend of the man came to offer a marriage proposal for his younger brother to a woman, who is beautiful and from a prestigious family, but she is divorced. The friend began to explain the reasons for the divorce until he revealed that she was wronged in her first marriage, which did not last for more than a month. The man interrupted him and rejected the whole proposal without thinking of consulting his brother. His friend argued, saying: "OK. Can you at least present the proposal to your brother? Maybe he has a different opinion." The man replied, "I am his older brother, and he has no opinion against my final words." After that, the man went to tell his brother proudly, but his younger brother scolded him, saying, "A man in my position and age doesn't need a guardian. This's the last time you speak on my behalf." The man replied to him, "I am your older brother, and I have a right over you." The brother said to him, "The only right that you have over me is the right of the brotherhood."

This example reveals the power enforcer has the tendency to act on behalf of others. Such tendency that makes him see himself worthy of acting on behalf of others and making decisions related to the core of their lives without consulting them.

- An uncle invited his nephew, on the occasion of his recent marriage, in addition to some relatives, to a club. When the waiter approached to take their orders, the uncle turned to the ladies and inquired, "What would you like to drink?" Each one answered what she wanted. But he looked at them in astonishment, then said to the waiter, "Bring them strawberry juice," while pointing at all the attendees, men or women, "and bring me coffee." Then he looked at the ladies, saying, "What a shame! Women don't get to choose. Their men are the ones to choose for them." While everyone just smiled.

This example illustrates the uncle's tendency to act on behalf of others, as he gave himself the authority to choose drinks for all the attendees, whether they were women or men, without consulting with any of them about their preferences. As if he was authorized by them to act on their behalf in choosing what they want.

- A college girl called her classmate at his house because she needed to review some lessons with him. And the mother answered her, without her son's knowledge, saying, "No! He is not here. Even if he is here, he is busy to speak to anyone." Then, she hung up.

There's no doubt that this mother fears for her college son to be corrupted by girls. Her fear for him prompted her to avert this danger. So she proceeded to act on his behalf to answer that girl's phone call in this way to keep her away from him.

Examples unfold in everyday situations, revealing the "tendency to act on behalf of others" is a trait of the power enforcer. For example:

- A man proposed to marry a widow who lived with her late husband's family. However, the brother of the deceased husband refused the proposal without consulting the widow, saying "Our women can only be with one man, and after him, they can only raise his children."

- A mother and daughter live together alone after the death of the father. When the girl got engaged, her cousin called her to schedule her fiancé's visits at times that suited his own availability, without asking for the girl's mother's permission. This was done so that he could be present during their visits to monitor their conversation.

-A man found his daughter and his brother's daughter sitting in the club with two young men, so he publicly hit them and then took his brother's daughter to her home and told her father - after telling him what had happened - "I hit her on your behalf." Now she is aware of the consequences of repeating such scandalous acts in the future."

- A father gave his blessing to a young man who proposed to his daughter without asking for her opinion. And when the young man argued, saying, "Well, are we going to ask the bride about her opinion? Maybe she has another opinion." The father replied, saying, "As long as I have made the decision and given you my word, that's all that matters. Everyone here agrees with me."

Perhaps the aforementioned positions revealed a trait of the power enforcer, which is the tendency to act on behalf of others.

3) Possessing Knowledge:

This is the third trait of the power enforcer, where the power enforcer sees himself as the legitimate heir of knowledge, so to speak, whether this knowledge is experience with life matters, or it is in any field of knowledge. As for the others, he thinks that they do not understand much, and therefore they deserve guidance and learning more from his knowledge and wisdom. Perhaps, in presenting some situations, we can clearly illustrate this trait:

- A brother, who is several months older than his younger brother, and despite this, the elder (senior) often deliberately imposes his views on his younger brother (junior), and directs his life and the life of his family. Until his younger brother got bored and order him to stop repeating this behavior. So the older brother replied to him, saying, "I am your big brother." The younger brother replied, "What's the deal with this "big brother" thing? You're just a couple of months older than me." The older brother replied, "You know the famous proverb; "He who is a day older than you knows more than you by a year."

This situation exemplifies the concept of how power enforcers assert their superiority through knowledge. The older brother insists on interfering in his younger brother's life, based on the belief that the elder always possesses greater experience and knowledge by virtue of their age, compared to the younger who always lacks experience and knowledge, regardless of how old they are or how much life experience they gain. This notion is well-expressed by the popular proverb.

- During class, a student asked her teacher about a piece of information, seeking clarification. Instead of verifying whether the student was correct or not, the teacher responded with, "It is unacceptable for a student like you to tell me that I'm wrong." I'm sure of what I've said is correct. It's also very shameful for you to check with your teacher, as you do not understand anything."

From the previous situation, we find that the stronger party in the relationship considers herself the only source of knowledge, and is the most knowledgeable and experienced, especially if the objecting party is younger than her. As the former party may act violently with the later and even mocking them and their knowledge.

Examples unfolds in everyday situations, emphasizing this trait of those who exercise power. For example;

A son criticizes the clothes his mother wears that are not appropriate for her age, saying, "It's a shame that you're wearing this dress, Mum. It's not appropriate for your age." The mother replied, "I think I am old enough to know what's right and wrong. I don't need any advice from anyone, especially from a kid like you who doesn't know anything about life. Save your advice for yourself."

- A patient went to two doctors specializing in the same field because he was suffering from an illness. One of the doctors told him that he needed to undergo surgery urgently. The patient was not convinced, so he went to the other, who told him that he did not need the surgery and that it would be enough to take the medicines. So the patient returned to the first doctor and confronted him with what his colleague said. He replied to the patient, "This person is not knowledgeable in the field of our specialization. I'm telling you is the right thing. If you don't like it, just go to him."

- An Islamic preacher frequently appears on a satellite channel to discuss sensitive and potentially dangerous religious issues. He gives direct on-air fatwas, either permitting or forbidding certain practices, without conducting any research or review. Despite this, he has never admitted to not knowing something. He speaks with unwavering confidence, using assertive language such as "This is forbidden (Haram)" or "It is not permissible", as if he is an authority on all matters of religion and life.

The situations mentioned above illustrate some of the traits that knowledgeable individuals possess. They tend to monopolize knowledge, take pride in it, and mock the knowledge of others, as if no one else knows what they know. Additionally, they often use assertive language, such as saying "I am right" or "I know what I'm saying." This reflects his inflated sense of knowledge possession, and therefore everything he says is correct and no one has the right to argue or check with him. Therefore, when the word 'shame' is directed at him, he rebels against it as he is accustomed to using it himself. In order to avoid the risk of appearing unknowledgeable in front of others, he behaves arrogantly and is reluctant to admit his mistakes, going so far as to feign knowledge to avoid being perceived as ignorant. And then; He is found torn between calling for knowledge and claiming it.

III- Mechanisms of Consolidating Power:

They are the mechanisms that a person resorts to in order to consolidate his power in everyday life. These mechanisms can be broken down into two mechanisms, namely; the encouragement mechanism and the prevention mechanism. In the following pages, I will try to explain and illustrate them!

1) Encouragement Mechanism:

It is the method used by the stronger party to encourage practices that are acceptable and appropriate to him and are consistent with his values and wishes. This method ranges between using expressions of encouragement and approval, to giving material rewards. Let us reflect on situations from our everyday lives to see how such person encourages practices that is consistent with him:

- A father encourages his young son to hit his sister, who is a few years older than him, telling him, "Good for you, son! Hit her again. Hit her over her head to obey you. Be a man."

The expressions of approval that the father resorted to with his son, and the words of encouragement they bear, reveal the divisive policy used by many parents when raising boys and girls. It is a policy derived from the vision that believes that the true man is the one who can control the woman, in order to raise and bring her up well. Therefore, the young son carries out this vision with his sister in order to be worthy of the words of encouragement and approval from the father, especially since he declared his early manhood, by doing this act. And for that he deserved the encouragement from the father.

- A young man asks his uncle's opinion about his intention to delay his sister's wedding due to the death of a relative. The uncle replied in support, "Good for you, son! There's no shame on you. Respecting other people's sorrows is our duty too. And we are supposed to be considerate of each other."

- A father and a mother are visiting a relative, and at exactly ten in the evening they are about to leave. However the host argued with them, saying, "It is still early. We didn't have enough time to sit down with each other." They replied, "It's hard for us to stay because we force the children not to be late. It would be unacceptable for us to order them not to be late while we get home late. In order for them to abide by our rules, we must adhere to them first."

However, the mechanism of encouragement does not stop at the limits of linguistic approval only. It goes beyond that to material encouragement as well. For example:

- A father tempts his son to succeed, and he tells him, "If you get a high GPA and attend the Faculty of Medicine, I will get you the car that you want."

- A mother asks her young son to be polite in the presence of guests, telling him, "You know, if you adhere to my orders and stop acting naughty, I will bring you sweets and a lot of toys."

In the light of the foregoing, we have seen the power enforcer resorts to the use of encouragement and approval at times, support and setting examples at other times, and reward at another time in order to encourage the practices that is consistent with him. Then comes the language that imposes power in this context, which is an encouraging language, through using expression like; "There's no shame on you!", "That's the right thing do!", "Good for you!"... etc. Although these expressions are not devoid of any trace of power. For in the situations between the father and his son, or the uncle and his nephew; the language was encouraging and supportive that was based on phrases such as; "Bravo!", "My dear son", "What a clever boy!" This language, through its vocabulary, reveals the nature of the relationship between the speaker and the listener, which is a vertical relationship. As the speaker of the previous phrases only directs them to those of lower status than him, or to those who are younger. Of course, he cannot use it with someone who is superior or his equal to him.

2) Prevention Mechanism:

It is the other mechanism used by the stronger party to prevent practices that are inconsistent with him and his desires. This mechanism revolves around two forms of power, which are the physical power, and the symbolic power. The aforementioned topics are described below.

A] Physical Power:

This form is represented in the direct power used by the stronger party to prevent practices that don't conform to his desires and will. There are many physical means that such person can resort to in everyday life, such as resorting to beatings, abandonment, and cursing and insults:

- A father beats his daughters with a stick to force them not to use mobile phones when they are outside the home.

- A father beats his son in the street, and another man comments, "This is the right way to raise him. He must break his son's neck in order to improve his manners. My father used to hit me with slippers and the gas cylinder hose. And I could not talk to him or do anything wrong."

- A wife deals with her husband sharply, with a loud voice, and strictness in order to prevent him from being irresponsible with the household and not caring about raising their children.

- A manager treats her subordinates seriously and strictly, and threatens to file complaints against the under-performers, so that her subordinates don't think her weak, and she could succeed in her work and controls the troublemakers.

- A husband quarrels with his wife, insults her in the street, and leaves her without getting her home, because a neighbor called her by her name without using titles.

- A woman got angry with her husband and left him, and refrains from talking to him for a few days, because she saw him talking to another woman.

- A mother rebukes her son who spilled the juice on his clothes, telling him, "Stop! What did you do? If you did this again, I will hit you"

- A teacher punished a student and prevented her from attending the class because she said to him, "I don't understand the lesson."

-A teacher caught a student cheating during an exam. In response, the teacher publicly scolded the student and made an example of him for the other students. Ultimately, the teacher decided to expel the cheating student from the exam room.

The physical means of the power enforcer varied between anger, beatings, scolding, rebuking with a loud voice, curses, insults and threats, abandonment, and expulsion. The power enforcer's language is also characterized by being a commanding language, and its vocabulary includes "Do...", "Do not...", "You must...", "Don't you ever...", "Be aware...", "Stop!" ,"Stay in your lane!", and "Shame on you!".

B] Symbolic Power:

It is represented by the indirect power, in which a person resorts to prevent practices that are inconsistent with him and his values. The symbolic power is not a power that imposes itself only through commands, but it's exercised without us having to exercise it. We can call it a natural authority and it inhabits language and behavior patterns. (Pierre Bourdieu, 1990, p. 77).

The following examples will try to reveal how a person can influence others by using symbols and what they provide as means of pressure on behavior:

An elderly woman was left standing on a train as she hadn't been able to secure a seat. She stood beside a man who was seated and asked him if he had any suggestions, as she couldn't stand the whole way. The man replied, "Madam, I have been standing since morning. I am tired and my legs are sore." Another passenger who was also standing interjected, "That's unacceptable (Haram)! Shame on you! She is an old lady." Then he turned to the woman and said, "If only I had a booked a seat, I would gladly offer it to you." This conversation forced the person setting on the chair to leave it to her.

This woman takes advantage of factors (such as age, illness, and gender) to influence others. It is shameful for a man not to stand up for an elderly woman, let alone if an elderly and sick woman. Respect for the elderly requires showing them courtesy by offering them a seat and inviting them to sit down. If someone does not respond, the elderly person may begin to exert pressure symbolically, by leveraging the concepts of shame, age, and illness as tools of influence.

- A manager went to her office and found in her reception some female employees who had come from the company's branch to approve some papers. She found the office unclean and the service worker absent. So she said, "Oh! The whole place is dusty. Apparently the cleaner is absent today. Now, I can't write over the desk in this way." (the female employees were standing silent)... And she continued, saying, "I will have to get any cloth to clean the desk with." Then she said sadly, "Oh, my knee hurts so much. Once I sat down, I could not get up quickly. But what can I do? I must stand up." At this moment, one of the female employees started to cleaned the desk with a paper napkin, while the manager tried to deter her, saying, "My girl, stop. I was about to stand up. I shouldn't let you work!"

We can notice that this woman gradually begins to exercise the symbolic power and put pressure on female employees. As she begins by describing the situation of the unclean office due to the absence of the service worker, then pointing out that she is unable to write on the desk while it is dusty, and implicitly indicated that she will not be able to get their papers approved, as a result. The pressure increased by drawing attention to her illness and the excruciating pain she would feel if she stood up suddenly. And the pressure continued until one of the female employees began to clean the desk instead of the absent office cleaner.

- A man and his wife went to a doctor's clinic after she had undergone surgery. Upon arriving, they found the clinic to be crowded and were unable to book an appointment in advance. The husband said to the patients, "Come on people, my wife is tired, and she's just undergone a surgery." A patient said to him, "So! We are all tired. You should wait for your turn, sir." The husband said to him, "Shame on you, man! She's a woman." He addressed the other patients in the clinic, saying "Whoever thinks that he deserves to enter and visit the doctor before a woman who's just undergone a surgery and wants to remove the surgery sutures, they can enter!" So everyone fell silent.

This situation reveals the great influence of the symbolic power, as well as what the word (shame) represents in terms of symbolic power that a person uses it in order to consolidate his power over others.

There are symbolic means that a woman can use to influence a man, using her gentle and affectionate style at times, and her tears and weakness at other times, in order to dissuade him from his position against her, and make him fulfill her desires without hesitation.

Among the symbolic means is also the insisting on requests, which we can see in the following example:

- A father refuses to let his daughter go out to attend her friend's birthday party, telling her, "It is late and you can't go out alone." So the daughter presses him, saying: "For God sake, dad! If you love me, let me go out. Or do you want to let me get upset? Aren't I your beloved daughter? If you love me, please agree."

Likewise, religion, which is one of the most widely used and influential symbolic means, is used by the power enforcer to influence others. Examples include:

-        A father disowned his daughter and refused to deal with her because she refused to marry her cousin. He also warned her of the divine punishment that awaits her for her disobedience.

-        A husband who doesn't want his wife to work tells her, "Your home and your children should come first." She insists on working, saying, "I'm tired of staying at home, and working won't affect my responsibilities at home." He tells her, "You are free to choose, but you should know that if you work, it will displease God because the Hadith says 'Obey your husband to obey the Lord', and you are disobeying me."

-        A doctor wants his son to join the Faculty of Medicine so that he can inherit the clinic after him. The son refuses and insists on studying engineering. His father tells him, "You should know that if you attend the faculty you want, you will still disobey me. And you know that our Lord commanded obedience to parents, because I raised you and I have rights over you."

-        A mother refuses to let her young son marry a divorced woman, so she says to him, "You know, my son, that I am sick. Do you want to kill me? You should know what if you went on with your decision and married this woman, then you will not be my son, and I'll disown you. And if something happens to me, it will be because of you."

Finally, body image and its associated attributes can be used as symbolic means to consolidate power. This includes growing a beard, having a prayer mark on the forehead, and carrying a rosary. Additionally, eloquent language, tone of voice, and speech manners are important factors. The use of classical Arabic, religious phrases, and quotes from the Quran and Hadiths can enable a speaker to communicate their message powerfully due to the inherent influence and power of the language.

It is evident from the previous examples of symbolic power that a person may resort to using symbolic means when lacking the legitimacy represented by direct material and physical power. The use of symbolic power arises from the uncommon representations of power, such as a woman imposing power over a man, a girl over her father, a son over his father, or a situation where an elderly woman is unable to book a seat on a train. These unconventional representations of power may result in a sense of illegitimacy, prompting individuals to rely on symbolic means to maintain their authority. And other examples that illustrated the use of symbols as a means of pressure on behavior in a way that achieves legitimacy that is far from using explicit orders.

There is a lingering question: after the dominant party, with their various mechanisms, successfully influences the behavior of others to align with their values, does this influence and success lead to the creation of stereotypes of submissiveness and compliance? Or is everyday life capable of creating different representations of submission?

Let us see in the next chapter how the submissive persons create forms or rather strategies of their submissiveness in everyday life.

4

How is the Submissive Self Shaped in Arab Culture?

I- Forms of Submission Everyday Life:

The term "submission" in this chapter refers to the act of an individual being subjected to the concept of shame and its implications within traditional cultural and social values. But how does a person submit in everyday life? By studying the situations of daily life, in an attempt to search for an answer to this question, we can identify four forms of those who are submissive to the traditional culture, namely:

1. Low-profile persons

2. Those who obey the speech authority

3. Those who blend with things

4. Those who are accomplices of the dominant

1) Low-profile persons:

They are people who are fully qualified to be submissive due to their position in the social structure, which makes them find comfort in peace and security and flee from rebellion or riots for fear of the oppression and punishment of the dominant. And this fear drives them to deliberately avoid attracting attention or publicity and to tend to keep a low profile in order to avoid problems or conflicts. The representations of these submissive people are numerous and varied, including women, men, and young people. Perhaps, by presenting some situations, we can clearly illustrate those submissive people:

- A service worker, in one of the public entities, can be seen as conservative in his dealings with the employees and accepts insults from the superiors with open arms. If he is asked about why he acts in this way, he replies, "People should not rise above their station. And I'm under their thumb."

- An employee in a high-ranking position strives to please their superiors by executing their orders with utmost precision and dreads any form of critique. They are also hesitant to express any objections to their superiors. If someone does criticize their negative behavior, the employee's response is, "Those who wish to maintain their position must turn a blind eye."

We have discovered that holding a high-ranking position does not necessarily confer power to its owner. In fact, it often results in the individual becoming more submissive and weaker due to the fear of losing their position. This fear sets boundaries for the submissive person and determines the issues over which they should not have conflicts with their superiors. As a result, the submissive person seeks to please their superiors and engages in practices that affirm their submission, such as bowing during greetings and avoiding eye contact while talking to their boss. Also, we see him agreeing and supporting everything his boss says, and this may apply equally to both the person in the high position and the simple employee. Both of them submit to preserve their jobs, and this fear drives them to walk, compelled, with their eyes and ears shut.

- An employee complained to her husband, a senior official in a security authority, about a quarrel that occurred between her and a colleague at work. The husband summoned him to his place of work (the security authority) terrorized and threatened him into not repeating what he had done with his wife again. When the colleague went to work, he told some of his colleagues about what happened to him. And they advised him to file a complaint with the department director against that employee and another complaint against her husband with his superiors and not to be afraid of him. He replied by saying, "No! I won't do that... It is better to evade his evil and the evil of his wife. He seems to be of a higher position and status. Better safe than sorry."

Thus, the representations of the submissive people in the previous situations reveal that their practice of submission stems from their position in the social structure. This is clearly expressed by the submissive words and phrases with which they express such a position, such as "Walking close to the wall (to turn a blind eye)." "People should not rise above their station.", and "Better safe than sorry." Therefore, we found them surrendering to the captivity of fear, which makes them flee from mere objection and refuse revolution for fear of the oppression and punishment of the dominant. And they express this by saying, "I'm under their thumb." "It's better to evade his evil.", "He seems to be of a higher position and status," and the other expressions that the submissive person may use.

Submission is not only restricted to men. It also includes women. For example:

- A husband orders his wife not to raise her voice when speaking to him. When she agreed, her mother-in-law supported her, saying, "May God bless you, my girl. A respectable woman listen to her husband's words. And whatever he says, she must act upon it, even over her dead body."

Submissiveness also includes young people. For example:

- A group of siblings submit to the authority of their father, who ordered them to sever their ties with their brother, who went against his order (will) by marrying someone who does not approve of. So the brothers submitted, saying, "It's none of our business. Why should we be at odds with him. Everyone is responsible for their acts and must face the consequences of their mistakes."

- A girl submits to her mother regarding choosing her clothes. As the mother imposes certain clothes on her and the girl cannot object or express her opinion. She says to her mum, "As you like, Mum."

- A young child submits to his father, who threatened to beat him if he went out and played in the street again. So the child told him fearfully, "OK. I won't do that again."

This observation highlights that the submissive person's fear of the dominant sets clear boundaries that they must not cross in order to gain their approval and support. This ultimately results in the submissive person turning a blind eye to negative behavior or actions.

2) Those who obey the speech authority:

What will people say? Submissive individuals often find themselves asking the question, "What will people say?" in various aspects of their lives such as when eating, dressing, speaking, laughing, or even loving. This question exposes the powerful influence that others' opinions and words have on them. The fear of being judged and criticized by others is pervasive, and everyone dreads the scrutiny and condemnation of their actions. Consequently, we observe submissive individuals willingly or unwillingly submitting and practicing subservience, in the hope that they will earn approval and acceptance from those around them. Perhaps, in presenting some situations, we can clearly illustrate this:

- A woman is urging her widowed neighbor to move on from mourning by suggesting that wearing black clothes is not necessary to express sadness. She says, "Come on, sister! It's been long enough, you don't need to keep wearing black. Sadness is in the heart, not in the clothes." The widow replied, "That would be shameful, my dear! People will slander and bad mouth me. They will say, "She must be seeing someone now, or she wants to get married!."

This example reveals the power and influence of people's words on the submissive persons. This indicated by this widow's insistence on wearing mourning clothes in order to prove to everyone that she continues to grieve for her husband and refuse to resume her life again.

- A father postponed his daughter's wedding due to the death of his cousin. So the groom waited until forty days passed since the funeral, then he went to the bride's father to set the wedding date. But the father refused to set a date for the wedding and said to him, "Why are you in such a hurry? My cousin just passed away, and you want me to hold a wedding ceremony. My family and others will slander and speak ill of me." That will a big shame on me. Nothing will be done before at least a year, my son."

- A married woman, who over the age of fifty, found that she was pregnant, spoke to her friend and said, "I'm thinking of aborting the baby. What will people say about me? What will my husband and children say about me? Is it possible for me to give birth at such age? What a shame and disgrace!"

Thus, the previous examples reveal the power of people's words that force the submissive person into submitting and cower under its weight. In the previous situations, a sentence caught my attention, which was said by some submissive persons and repeated in more than one situation. It is "People will slander and bad mouth us," (lit. in Arabic: People will eat our face). What a harsh expression! It makes me wonder about the nature of the relationship between the submissive person and the people; And where did people get that power from? And why do the submissive persons care for these cannibals? Perhaps, by reviewing the rest of the situations, we can reveal the secret of that relationship.

- During a trip with colleagues and acquaintances, a man of high position was invited to a night-out party with entertainment activities. However, he declined the invitation, citing concerns about his image and status in the eyes of others. "I can't," he said. "What would people say if they saw me there? It would be a shame. You can go without me, and I'll watch from afar."

- A male colleague flirted with his female coworker by sending messages on her mobile phone containing sexual hints and inappropriate phrases. When her colleague advised her to report him to the manager, she refused, out of concern for her reputation and said to her, "People won't believe the truth, and they will surely say that I encouraged him to behave like that. Or else, how dare he do that? They'll accuse me. And I will be the one who is harmed and slandered at the end."

- A girl refused to marry a man younger than her. She said to those who offered his proposal to her, "People will make fun of me when they know that he is younger than me."

- A girl refused to marry a handicapped young man, saying, "If people accept him, they will definitely say there is something wrong with her. That's why she accepted it."

- A man refuses to marry a girl just because her sister is divorced and lives alone by herself, leaving her family home. He said, "What would I say to people when they ask me about my wife's sister? Why is she living alone by herself? And why is she away from her family's house?"

- A group of rural female students at the university refuses to talk to their male colleagues for fear of people's words. As this act will affect their reputation. And perhaps their families might hear about it and they will be subjected to the most severe types of punishment.

This is a sample of situations that reveal the submissive person's fear of people's words. Accordingly, they take actions willingly, and maybe they are not totally convinced of them, in order not to fall prey to people's words.

The previous situations have made it clear to me that most of the submissive individuals, regardless of their level, belong to the educated middle class. This can be attributed to the fact that the middle class places great importance on maintaining a clean and respectable image in front of others. The reason for this is that society grants this class a privileged and social position in order for them to bear the burden of preserving the customs and traditions of society. Hence, if the people of that class fail to carry out their previous duties; society and its members have go after them and held them accountable, which will result in lowering their position and social status. In turn, this will result in making every individual seeking to maintain his image and appearance by living as the other people want. The evaluations and opinions of others play a crucial role in determining and shaping one's sense of self. As a result, many individuals may submit to the group in order to gain their approval and appreciation. Paradoxically, this act of submission allows them to regain their sense of power and derive it from their connection to the group. It's expressed in Figure (6).

3) Those who become familiar with things:

Becoming familiar with something means getting used to it and practicing it without awareness or thinking. William James clearly expressed this meaning when he said, "Becoming familiar with things causes a sense of their plausibility. And then this sense of familiarity will serve as an intellectual tranquilizer." (Parenti, Michal, 1978, p45).

As I read through the everyday situations, I couldn't help but notice a common representation of submission. It struck me that many of those who unconsciously engage in acts of submission are not necessarily being instructed by an authority figure on what they should or shouldn't do. Instead, they submit as a result of habit and familiarity with certain behaviors or expectations. There is no doubt that this type of submissive persons has been subjected, at some time to, a power that imposed actions on them and dictated how to practice them. Therefore, they submitted to this power and practiced actions based on its determination. As time passes and they continue to repeat the behavior, it becomes ingrained and automatic, without conscious awareness or consideration.

Perhaps, in a presenting some situations, we can clearly explain what I've mentioned before:

- A young man crosses his legs while watching TV at home. Once his father enters, the young man puts his leg down and sits straight.

This example perfectly illustrates the concept of submission through familiarity. The father's authority in his home has made it necessary for his children to sit up straight in his presence from an early age. Through repetition, this act has become a habit that they do without even thinking about it. This behavior continues to develop and becomes ingrained in them through practice until it becomes second nature.

- A little girl fell to the ground and was injured. Soon, she extended her hand to cover with her dress a part of her small body, which was exposed by the air after the fall.

This example sheds light on the numerous taboos and restrictions imposed on a woman's body from a young age, as well as the consistent abuse she faces from her family whenever a part of her body is exposed. This is demonstrated by the child's immediate response to cover the exposed part of her body without paying attention to any injuries or wounds she may have. And then this turned into a behavior practiced by the girl, despite her young age, without thinking or being aware of.

- A girl was watching TV with her family. When a romantic scene appeared, the girl looked down, and a family member changed the channel until the scene ended.

- A group of young people at the university were smoking cigarettes in the classroom, and when their professor entered the lecture class, they put out their cigarettes immediately.

- In a rural family, women prepare food for the men first, and then they gather in a closed area to eat their food.

- A woman was sitting next to her husband in the passenger seat, and they were going to pick up a relative of the husband with them. And as soon as this relative appeared, the wife got out, of her own accord, from the car to give way to the passenger seat for the relative, and she sit in the back."

Perhaps these and previous examples indicate that those who get familiar with things are subject to the prevailing culture and its customs and traditions. But their submission is done unconsciously. Or rather, it become a habit and familiar thing.

4) Those who accomplice of the dominant:

The previous forms of submissiveness that I discussed include imposed obedience, low-profile behavior, fear of others' evaluations and submission to their words, and habitual submission that leads to familiarity between the submissive person and the act of submission. However, the discussion here is about another form of submission, which may be related to the previous forms of submissiveness. It's the result of deep-rooted cultural beliefs. This form assumes the existence of some kind of complicity between the submissive and the dominant persons. We find that the submissive person adopts the point of view of the dominant and makes the relationship between them seem normal (Pierre Bourdieu, 2001, p. 39). This complicity contributes to more submission on behalf of the submissive person and more authority for the dominant person. Perhaps, in presenting some situations, we can clearly illustrate this.

- In a conversation between some co-workers about the seriousness and strictness of their manager at work, one of them said, "As people, cordiality doesn't work for us. And if we did not use seriousness, we would not do anything. The boss must be firm and strict in order for us to follow his orders to the heart. He must get us treading on a tightrope."

This (submissive) speaker expresses the idea of complicity with the dominant. As he adopted the point of view of the dominant and made the manager's seriousness and strictness with the employees a useful medicine for them. For the employees, in his vision, (cordiality doesn't work for them), and there is a need for some seriousness and strictness (get them treading on a tightrope).

- A girl was talking to her fiancé on the phone, telling him, "I am going out now to visit my friend." Her fiancé replied, "You are free to do what you want." She replied in astonishment, "You are supposed to be in charge of me now. If you really loved me, you would have controlled me and told me I shouldn't go out without your permission. In addition, you should have asked me who this friend is, where did I got to know her, and what is my relationship with her?"

This girl considers her fiancé's control over her life as an ideal image of the nature of the relationship between men and women, which necessitates the man's absolute control over the woman. And she consider this an evidence of his love and interest in her.

- Two women were sitting in a balcony. A girl, who was wearing short clothes, passed by on the street. One of them commented, "Do you see what I see?" The other replied, "Is it possible that there is a man who has control over her?" The first woman replied, "I don't know what happened to men! If a man doesn't snarl, yell and hit his women, he wouldn't be a man."

This example expresses the stereotypical representation of men in the prevailing culture. This representation thinks that a true man only reprimands women and disciplines their behavior. The strange thing is that this form is the accepted one among a wide segment of women. These two women complied with the (dominant) man. Hence, it is normal for them to consider a man a true man when he (snarls and yells), otherwise (he will not be a man).

However, the accomplices are not satisfied with their complicity only with the dominant. Rather, they add a value to their submission to the dominant; a value that contributes to giving more control over them. Thus, it takes away from them the duty of submission without feeling it's submission, by relying on socially ingrained beliefs. (Pierre Bourdieu, 1425 AH, p. 223). The following two situations will explain this:

- A woman complains to her mother about the mistreatment of her husband who beats and insults her before her children and neighbors. And she has no means to react to him other than crying. The mother replied, "What is wrong with this, my girl? He is a man, and he must do that. And then, you're a good girl for not reacting to him. A good-natured woman must endure and be patient for the sake of her home and her children."

Thus, contentment with humiliation becomes evidence of good nature, good upbringing, and dedication to the upbringing of children. The qualities to which the mother added value was her daughter's silence and submission to her husband's violence and cruelty toward her. In the same time, they are the qualities that make him a man according to the fixed stereotype of men in the prevailing culture.

- A young unmarried girl was approached by a relative who proposed a marriage arrangement with a family for her. The relative described the girl as a good-natured, decent person who would make an excellent housewife. The relative also emphasized the girl's gentle and meek nature, assuring the family that she wouldn't argue or confront their son. The groom's mother replied, "Yeah. The important thing is that she be polite and gentle." The relative replied, "As for politeness, she is very polite, meek, and wants to just live in peace."

In the previous example, the woman lists the advantages of the girl to the family of the expected husband, highlighting that she is "polite, meek, gentle, a decent girl, and wants to just live." Meekness becomes a value added to the girl's advantages, while the rest of the mentioned traits act as a warranty that guarantees the future husband's ability to control her without any complaints on her part. Hence, those values contribute to more submissiveness and oppression of the person.

II: The suffering of the submissive persons:

The representations of submissiveness we have explored may be viewed as an oppression of behavior, whether it is externally imposed by societal powers or internally inflicted through habitual practices that the submissive individual becomes accustomed to over time. These practices can eventually evolve into a form of oppressive power over the individual. However, it begs the question of how submissive individuals feel towards such practices that oppress them. Are they content with them, or do they suffer as a result of their submission? What is the cost of such submission? Let us examine some everyday situations and consider the suffering that submissive individuals may experience.

- A woman travels daily to her workplace in another governorate by public bus. If she finds herself sitting next to a man, she will often roll her body into a small area of her seat so as not to touch the body of the man sitting next to her. She may continue sitting in this position for more than two and a half hours, while the man next to her sits upright in his seat, filling his chair completely.

This situation is not as simple and unassuming as it may seem. This woman is clearly submissive, and her submission causes her a great deal of suffering as she endures an intolerable position for over two and a half hours. This situation may be a common occurrence during her daily commute, as she strives to ensure that her body does not touch that of the man beside her, all without uttering a single word. Yet, if she were to speak up, the entire situation could be resolved. Meanwhile, the man next to her sits comfortably and without concern for her discomfort.

- In a verbal altercation between a couple, it ended with the wife insulting her husband and slapping him across the face, leaving the marital home and going to her family's home. Her justification for this altercation was that her husband abused her, but she did not disclose her abuse against him. When she stayed with her family for a long time, with her husband's refusal to come to end the dispute, her family and his family began attempts to reconcile the dispute. So a relative of the husband went and said to him, "You can't leave your wife with her family all this time. What happened to make her leave the house?" The husband feared for his general appearance and image in front of his relative, and he did not disclose the reason, and said, "Nothing happened. It's a normal quarrel. The relative replied, "Alright. As long as it's simple issue, don't let the shame be on you! Let the evil thoughts go away and let's go to her family to reconcile with her." And he kept pressuring the husband until he agreed with him and went to his wife so that no one would know the real reason for the dispute.

Undoubtedly, the husband in this situation is facing a great deal of suffering. He is afraid of how his family perceives him and wants to maintain his image in their eyes. This fear has led him to reconcile with his wife, even though she was the one who wronged him. He did so to prevent anyone from finding out the real reason behind the dispute, which could expose him to shame and embarrassment. In short, he had no other choice but to swallow his pride and reconcile with his wife to protect his image and reputation.

- A girl, who is about forty years old and has not been married yet, and suffers from the cruelty of people's words about her, to the point that they called her; a spinster, prude, and old maid... etc. A widower, who is in his mid-fifties with two children, proposed to marry her, and he is less than her academically. It didn't take long for her to think and reject him. So her mother rebuked her, saying, "How could you reject him? Do you think you're still young who has the right to accept or reject grooms. Remember, how old you are now!" The girl replied to her, "But this is less than me in everything, and his social status is not suitable for me… I do not want to marry him and then regret it." The mother replied, "You are supposed to thank God that that he accepted to propose to you in the first place at this age. This is ingratitude, if you don't accept him." So the girl was forced to accept the marriage proposal.

It is clear from the previous situation that some words have power over a person, such as "What do people say?", "ingratitude". These words have the power to shackle a person's freedom with regard to choosing, rejecting, and accepting. And they make him suffer whether he accepts or rejects what's impose on him. This girl suffers from the harshness of people's words outside her home, and the harshness of her family's words inside her home because of her old age and not being married. This cruelty that the girl suffers is derived from the prevailing culture that looks suspiciously at the girl who hasn't been married till an older age. As this allows others to search for the reasons for her blatant delay in marriage. Then, when an opportunity for marriage comes to her, and it is often an inappropriate one, the girl is subjected to pressure from her parents, who are suffering as well, until she accepts such proposal.

- A sick woman asked a friend of hers to bring a housemaid to clean her house. So the friend set an appointment for her to bring her. One day before the appointment, the patient cleaned a part of the house herself. When her daughter learned this, she denounced what her sick mother had done, saying, "Oh, mum! What did you do? You are sick and tired. Tell me why then will we bring a housemaid?" The mother replied, "I was trying to make the house look reasonable a bit. Do you want the strange woman to enter the house and find dirty like this? She will exposes us to the other people and they talk about us."

However, the everyday situations reveals that the submissive person can suffer as a result of being subject to shame in his daily interactions with people. For example, I find the submissive person, in some situations, is forced to compliment someone that he does like for fear of getting into trouble with anyone, eat food that he does not like, get embarrassed that he would kiss a person with a skin disease or who has a cold, preferring to harm his body over embarrassing others, or suppress his feelings of severe pain, feeling ashamed of showing it in front of people.

But the question now is; will the submissive person continue to submit and then suffer as a result of such submission? Or are there attempts by the submissive person to alleviate his suffering? This is what the next section will try to provide an answer for.

III- Submission Strategies:

The scope of this research is directed to those who feel suffering due to their submission to the traditional culture and seek then to find a way out of that suffering. This is not only represented by their resistance to traditional culture. Social action may be more complex than simply obeying or rebelling against a rule. Rather, the quest of these submissive persons is to create a strategy for their submission.

According to Bourdieu's description, a strategy is formed when a "practice" occurs at the convergence of a field with a living environment and a particular type of capital that is defined by the field. It is this capital that directs the scope of the strategy, and then the strategy always tries to create a sense of harmony between the practices and the capital to be obtained. This is almost the meaning that I meant about the strategy. However, Bourdieu's concept of strategy is more extensive than the specific meaning I adopted; to which the submissive person resorts to alleviate his suffering. To explain this, I say; the submissive person knows that submission to the traditional culture and its rules leads to an increase in his symbolic capital with the community. Therefore, in order to preserve this capital, all his practices submit to that culture so that the submissive person obtains the support of the community and gives a good impression of him to others.

However, the suffering that the submissive person feels as a result of his submission creates a conflict for him between submission to the traditional culture and its rules imposed on him, and the desire to resist it, which will result in his loss of his symbolic capital that he has always preserved. Hence, the submissive person creates a strategy to practice submissiveness in everyday life that tries to create harmony between his submission to the traditional culture and obtaining the capital expected from such submission, and managing the individual's desires and interests that may conflict with that culture.

That is strategy to the submissive person resorts to alleviate his suffering from submission to traditional culture. Yet, we can find that it drowns him in more submission, burdens and suffering. However, it is an optional suffering that he resorted to as a compromise that get him a release from the suffering imposed on him by that culture. Another form of submission emerges from this strategy, in which the submissive person resorts to trying to reconcile traditional culture with his desires and interests that may conflict with this culture. But he has to apply this strategy openly in front of others only. Hence he is not just submissive but rather, "acting-submissive". And by that I mean pretending to be submissive. I'll discuss in the following pages this issues "acting-submissive, while shedding light on the nature of his language because of its vital role in his strategy.

The Strategy of Acting Submissively:

A "acting-submissive" person strives to preserve his symbolic capital; This is evident in his keenness to emphasize his good reputation, and his preservation of the community's ethics and traditions, which qualify him to earn the respect of the community and its individuals and grant him the appreciation he deems appropriate. Therefore, he acts submissively, before others, to the community's culture, customs and imposed rules. This is normal since the acting-submissive person has appointed the society a judge on his behavior and a main source of evaluation. This, in a nutshell, is the strategy of acting submissively

But there remains a question, which is: How does the acting-submissive person create his strategy by which he preserves his capital in society? Perhaps, we can find in everyday situations an answer to this question:

- A man had a loud shouting quarrel with his wife who works as a manager in a government department when he saw on her mobile phone numbers with men's names, saying to her: 'Who are these people, Madame Sayed, and what are they saying?'" The wife defended herself, saying, "What are you saying? You know that they are the heads of the division in my department." The husband replied, while he is foaming in anger, "This is not my business. Shame on you, Madam, for keeping male contacts on your phone without asking your husband's permission." The wife replied, "Shame on you for saying this to me after all this time. Then again, don't you know the nature of my work and that I might need them for work?" The husband replied, "I don't care about your work at all. These contacts must be deleted immediately. Otherwise, I will break the phone over your head." And because the wife does not have the right to go against her husband, she resorted to a trick. She renamed the male contacts as female one. so he became Sayed (Sayeda), Fawzi (Fawzia), and Muhammad (Hamidah). In this way, the problem with her husband was resolved.

As it is clear, the interests of this wife at work require that she keep the contacts of her male colleagues on her mobile phone because her work requirments. But she is unable to keep these contacts so as not to go against the orders of her husband, who forced her to delete them. And to get out of this dilemma, she resorted to a trick, which is changing the male contacts into female ones. Thus, her husband calmed down as he was reassured that his orders would be carried out, and that his wife would not go against him. In the meanwhile, her work would proceed normally without any problems, with her complete conviction that she is not doing anything wrong.

- A man always quarrels, insults and curses his wife, who is always silent and does not object to what he does to her. And if he ordered her to do something, she only replies with (OK). One day her neighbor asked her, "Why do you always keep silent when he humiliates you like this? He is supposed to respect you a little bit, at least in front of your children." She replied to her neighbor, saying, It's just fine. I don't want more quarrels and suffering. What does he want? To just say OK. and fine. An OK. makes things go easy. My only wish is to enjoy a life free of conflict, and later, I can do what I want."

In this situation, the wife, who may appear weak, has developed a strategy to confront her strong husband. She outwardly presents herself as submissive to her husband's will, obediently carrying out his desires and seemingly content with a lifestyle based on violence and abuse. Her strategy involves relying on silence and simply saying "OK" to her husband's demands. However, this approach has given her the false belief that she is content with her life, as she justifies her actions by saying "An OK makes things go easy" and "My only wish is to enjoy a life free of conflict"

- A young man proposed to a girl. And since this young man has a brilliant future ahead, he was accepted by the family and got its blessing. However, they asked him to get their daughter a very expensive bridal jewelry, so that she would be equal to those of her relatives who had preceded her in marriage, which the young man was unable to do. So he rejected the condition because of his inability to pay a bridal jewelry half the value of the requested. However, the family rejected this value, explaining the reason, by saying, "It's not possible. What would we say to people and our relatives?" The young man almost withdrew, apologizing for his proposal to the girl. At this point, the girl's father found a solution to this problem, which is for the young man to buy a bridal jewelry as much as he can for the girl. in the meanwhile, he can rent another expensive bridal jewelry for the girl to wear in front of her family and friends at the engagement ceremony, and then return it to the jeweler.

Thus, the fear of people's words pushed this family to resort to this solution, or rather a strategy, which made it preserve its general appearance and image, or its symbolic capital in front of others, and at the same time ensured that the young man is kept as a husband for the girl.

There are numerous examples in everyday situations that reveal the strategies of the acting-submissive. For example:

- A girl who is liberal in her dress code and manner of speaking, which made her neighbors slander her reputation and expose her to everyone who proposed to marry her, which made those who proposed to marry her refrain from doing so because of her bad reputation. And when a relative of her family offered a suitable man who worked in a prestigious position, the family was at a loss, because their daughter's reputation would prevent her marriage to him. So the family reached a solution, which is to change their place of residence by moving to a new residence in order to escape from the tongues of their former neighbors. And they also ordered their daughter to wear modest clothes and to wear loose-fitted Abayas.

- A man loves his colleague at work, and she shares the same feelings for him. However, they were afraid to show this affection in order to avoid the tongues of their colleagues until their official engagement. So the man would ignore her in front of their colleagues, or may abuse her verbally sometimes in order to divert minds from the possibility of a relationship between them. Yet, he treats the rest of her female colleagues in a normal way.

- A man always called his female relative by her pet name. And when he got married, he made sure to call his female relative by her real name, in the presence of his wife, in order to avoid problems with his wife.

- A man does not perform the prayers, but he was keen on performing the Friday Congregational Prayers only in the mosque. And he justifies that to his wife, saying, "I have to attend Friday prayers every week because people may have a bad idea of a person who does not pray."

- A college girl whose colleague gave her an romantic letter explaining his feelings and admiration for her, So the girl rebuked and criticized him loudly in front of their colleagues. Then she tore up the letter and threw it on the ground, saying to him, "Shame on you for disrespecting your colleague by doing what you did." After everyone left, she collected the letter and read it.

Perhaps these and previous examples reveal that the acting-submissive person does not rebel against the traditions of his society. Rather, he is submissive who is prompted by the conflict of his submission with his desires and interests to attempt to reconcile them. And that attempt is the strategy.

Perhaps it would be reasonably to talk here about the language of submission because of its close connection with the strategy. As language is the tool used by both the submissive and the acting-submissive persons in those attempts to reconcile. Therefore, it is necessary to shed light on language strategies.

Language Strategies:

Perhaps, upon careful consideration of the languages of the submissive and the acting-submissive persons, one will realize what they contain of prohibition and reservations when they interact with others. The language of the submissive person is characterized by being neutral, anxious, and bound by the shackles of shyness and fear of doing wrong and being stigmatized as shameful.

So language creates strategies by which it attempts to reconcile the authority of traditional culture with the desires and interests of both submissive and the acting-submissive persons. This language is distinguished by its reliance on various methods, which can be summarized in two methods. The first one is something that we can borrow the term Bourdieu coined for it, which is [kindness of expression]. And by this, I mean the submissive person resorts to using linguistic expressions that are kinder than the words and expressions that he must use in order to mitigate the impact of his words on others. As for the second method; it is the acting-submissive person's use of (protective words) to prevent being misunderstood by others. Perhaps, in presenting examples of that language from the everyday situations, I can explain what I mentioned in general:

a) Kindness of Expression

- A woman asks her relative what she thinks of her baby girl. She asks her, while smiling, "What do you think of her?" The relative replied, "She's not pretty. But she's funny."

- A group of employees went with their manager at work on a recreational trip to an amusement park. They gathered around a dangerous game, and their manager refused to participate with them, claiming that he's afraid, saying, "No. You are free to go. I am very coward." Then one of the employees replied to him, saying, "Excuse me, sir! what cowardice are you talking about? You don't have the needed amount of courage."

- A woman was talking to her female friend about the morals and merits of a colleague of theirs at work. Then her friend said to her, in wicked way, "If anyone hears you talking about him, they would say that you love him." The first one got flustered and said, "No. I love him! The whole thing is that I only cherish and respect him."

Thus, these examples reveal that the submissive person, when he feels anxious and afraid of the reaction of others to his speech, he resorts to create a language that is lighter in impact on others. And this is evident when his language depends on negating the good quality instead of mentioning the bad quality. The expression (not pretty) is much gentler than (ugly or hideous), and also (has no courage) is less blunt than (coward), and (cherish) is lighter than the word (love).

- A woman went to the gynecologist and explained to him what she is complaining about in colloquial language, and when she mentioned everything related to the female issues she used the Modern Standard Arabic.

- A group of saleswomen were displaying women's clothing in a public authority to a group of female employees. And when it comes to talking about the undergarments and inquiring about its quality, the female employees would say their names in English.

As can be seen, these two situations show that the submissive person is resorting to Modern Standard Arabic or a foreign language to utter some words that he is ashamed to mention publicly in the colloquial language that he may consider, at times, to be a vulgar language.

b) Protective Words:

- A man speaks affectionately with a female relative of his, who is in the prime of her life and is several years younger than him, about the need for her to think about early marriage, and urges her to do so. His wife interrupted his speech, smiling and saying, "It seems that care so much for her." The man hastened to say, "She's like my daughter. It's natural that I care about her."

- A man was speaking to a woman in full view of others, using the plural form and saying, "What are you doing? We really missed you. We want to see you soon."

- A woman talks to a man on the phone from her workplace, in the middle of her male and female colleagues, using a female pronoun and saying, "How are you? How is your mum? I want to see you." And none of her colleagues knew that she was talking to a man except for her best friend, who was sitting smiling.

In light of the above; we find the people in the previous situations have used words and voices to protect them from others' misunderstanding and words against them, or at least to divert the thoughts away from them. There is no doubt that the man addressing the woman in the plural form, and sometimes in the masculine form as well, or the woman addressing the man in the feminine voice, or the use of the word (my daughter), provided ultimate protection to them from the others.

However, in the lower levels of society, they use protective phrases or words such as the word (Excuse me!) and then utter whatever words and phrases they want, some of which are outright obscene, and some of them use it with the intention of not getting misunderstood. So the use of the word (Excuse me!) is serves as conduit to a what comes after it, whether words, phrases and sentences that are mentioned very easily and automatically, in order to protect the speaker from any blame or reproach. We find that this word can loosen the restrictions of the language as if the speaker had taken an implicit permission from the listener to say anything after that (without being accused of anything).

These were some of the strategies used by the submissive and the acting-submissive persons in their daily interactions with others in order to preserve their symbolic capital in society.

Having said that, I've talked about shame and the perceptions about it, its subjects, its uses, its enforcers, and those who are subject to it. But there remains a question remains, which is; Is there resistance against the concept of shame? I hope we will find the answer to this question in the next chapter.

5

How is the Resistant Self Shaped in the Arab Culture?

I: Forms of Resistance in Everyday Life

Upon examining life situations carefully, we can recognize two main forms of resistance, which demonstrate the nature of those who resist shame and traditional culture, and reveal the extent of their relationship to power. The first form is swimming against the tide, while the second form is having faces without masks. Perhaps, in presenting some scenes from the everyday life, we can reveal these two images.

1) Swimming Against the Tide:

These resisting persons are distinguished by their ability to resist and defy the traditional culture. As this culture seeks to subjugate and frame them within the framework of its concepts and customs. And they draw this resistance on their rejection and lack of conviction in many of the concepts of that culture, because it is, in their view, contradictory and inconsistent. As a result, they resist shame and challenge prevailing traditions, despite any powers that may stand in their way. This defiance poses a question that may not have crossed the minds of many submissive individuals - why is shame considered shameful? They ask this question first of themselves and then of society, as they seek to challenge and push back against established norms. Hence, their resistance is conscious and intentional, defiant and indifferent to the power imposed on them.

When we examine everyday situations more closely, we can identify the reasons why someone might decide to swim against the tide and break free from the traditions they have grown tired of and resist. These reasons can be grouped into three main components: the invalidity of shame, the desire to fly, and preserving the Status.

The following situations may explain these reasons and their manifestations.

a) Invalidity of Shame:

Individuals who swim against the tide are convinced that traditional practices are outdated, invalid, and lack logic and reasoning. Therefore, they reject these practices and stand against them, armed with reasoning to support their position. This is evidenced by the following situations:

- A girl once caught her mother smoking, despite having always been told that it was shameful for a girl to hold a cigarette. In response, the girl asked her mother, "Why do you smoke, Mum? Cigarettes are harmful." Her mother replied sharply, "I am old, but you are still young." The girl then questioned her mother, "Does smoking become shameful only for the young and not for the old?"

We often scrutinize and accuse our children of being inexperienced and unaware, forgetting that they may have a stronger and more reasonable logic than ours. We even de-legitimize their logic when we contradict ourselves by saying one thing and doing another. This mother set the standard for her daughter by dictating what is considered shameful or harmful. However, she failed to uphold her own standards when her daughter questioned her actions, revealing the contradiction between her words and actions. The mother had previously told her daughter that smoking was shameful and harmful, yet she herself smoked. So she deserved her daughter's scrutinization. Yet, the mother, who is accustomed to criticizing and directing her daughter, and not the other way around, was only open to exercise her power over her daughter, where she can assign to herself the position of power and guidance in the house. She embodied this concept by saying, "I am old, but you are still young." But the mother did not realize that her response created a sharp contradiction between her statements and actions, which led her daughter to question her mother's credibility and the concept of shame that the mother used, which is proved to lack credibility.

- A private tutor went to a student's home to give him a private tuition class with a group of students. Before the start of the lesson and while waiting for the students to come, this conversation took place between the teacher and the student. The teacher said, "Tell me, what did you eat for lunch today?" The student replied, "I ate chicken, rice, and potatoes." After class, the mother admonished her son, saying, "Son, it is shameful to tell someone what we ate for lunch. These are private affairs. You must learn not to spill the secrets of our home to anyone." The student was taken aback by his mother's admonition and replied in astonishment, "But what was I supposed to say when he asked me what I had for lunch? Should I have told him I don't know? Is there anyone who doesn't know what he would eat for launch. Do you want the teacher to think that I am an idiot?" The mother remained silent and did not speak.

Even though the example is simple and amusing, it illustrates the resistance of those who defy tradition when they see no logic in feeling ashamed. The child in this case was not convinced that sharing the dishes he had for lunch was something to be ashamed of. Hence, the mother couldn't find a proper response to her son except silence. Shame needs to present a strong reasoning for this child too. Otherwise, why is it considered shameful? In this case, the shame argument must be silenced forever.

Let us review other examples in which we see that shame lacks its reasoning before the resisting persons:

- A brother admonishes his older brother when he saw him coming home late at night, when he was the one who always prohibited him from coming home late. So he said to him, "So, why were you telling me that it is a shame to stay out late till midnight? In the same time, you come home at such hour!"

- A young woman was trying to book her aunt a bus ticket when she was travelling with her. The aunt objected, saying, "No! I swear, I can't have that. That would be a shame! Then, who is the older one among us?" The younger woman smiled and said, "It's much simpler than being about shame and age. It's not a big deal."

- A teacher rebukes a student in an exam class whom he saw chewing gum, saying, Shame on you, girl! Take that gum out your mouth." His colleague replied, "Come on! what's wrong about it? As long as she is sitting quiet and writing her answer in the exam papers. What's the problem? Maybe the gum helps her concentrate and solve the test."

- A neighbor returned to her neighbor some things that she borrowed from her. the later one refused to take them back, saying, "Come on! That would be a shame! I will not take anything." The former one replied, "Nothing shameful about it. I can't take these things for free. If you borrow something from me and come to me to return them, I will not be ashamed to take them back."

- A family resists customs and accepts that its daughter marry without organizing a wedding ceremony, or buying luxurious furniture, which they consider to be outdated traditions. And the family doesn't care about the opinions of their extended family and friends who have been dominating and controlling them.

Thus, the previous examples reveal that resistance occurs to the resisting person when shame loses its meaning and reasoning, and then he sees submission to this concept as illogical action.

b) Desire to fly:

Those who swim against the tide resist the concept of shame, due to their unbridled desire for freedom and to fly away and escape the shackles of the concept that seeks to enchain them to the traditional culture. Therefore, we find them resisting any power that could stand in the way of their freedom. Perhaps, in presenting some situations, we can clearly illustrate this:

- A woman who lives freely without being subject to any authority. That's why she is used to returning home late, wearing what she likes even if it contradicts people's opinions, in addition to talking to whoever she wants without restrictions or reservations. When her mother drew her attention to the fact that she needs to change her behavior for fear of people's words, she replied, "I don't do anything wrong. I don't care about people. I live my life the way I want."

This woman refuses to give up her freedom to any power, even if such power is as big as people's words, which have a magical effect on the behavior of individuals. Despite this, she insists on living her life the way she deems right, without caring about anyone, or allowing anyone to direct her life in a direction she does not want. So she wears what she likes and not what people like, and she goes out and comes back home whenever she wants, without any reservations.

- A service worker at a school went on a trip organized by her school administration with her students. She put on kohl on her eyes and kept singing, dancing and laughing with the female students. This caught the attention of the male and female teachers who were supervising the trip, that they asked her sarcastically, "What are you doing to yourself?" She replied indifferently, "It's once in a blue moon when I get to do this. Let me have fun and stop worrying!"

This worker is suffering under the weight of social restrictions imposed on her as a natural result of her social status on the one hand, and the nature of her life on the other hand. Then, she finally had the opportunity to cast off the burden of restrictions and express her love for life and desire for freedom, even if only for a short while.

- A group of young people were living freely in terms of their clothes, language, and general appearance. Whenever their families reminded them of the need to follow the societal norms regarding dress code, language, and appearance, they responded with sarcasm and irony, saying things like "Anyone who disapproves of this should mind their own business. We are not doing anything wrong, and we don't hurt anybody. So, why are they interfering with our life?"

These young men are openly challenging a social tradition, which is expressed clearly in an Egyptian proverb that can be literally translated into English as follows: "Eat whatever you like and wear whatever people like," not paying attention to what might be said about them. It is their desire to fly away to gain their freedom, and their explicit rejection of social stereotypes, whether from society or family that subject many under their weight. Thus, they went on to defy all social traditions in terms of their dress code, language, and general appearance.

There are many examples of those flying away seeking their freedom, which are indicative of their behavior in life. For example:

- A girl resisted the authority of her elder sister who objected to her way of dressing, which relied on short clothing and bold makeup, saying, "You are not my guardian. I'm not a little girl. I am free."

- A young woman desires to get engaged to her co-worker who is also young. When he proposed to her, her family rejected him citing a lack of social equality between them. The young woman persisted in marrying her colleague despite her family's objections and was not concerned about their boycott.

- A fifty-year-old widow defied her family and children when she decided to marry a young man twenty years younger than her, arguing that she had the right to love and live her life.

- A college girl from Upper Egypt firmly refuses to marry her cousin, who dropped out, despite her father's abusive attempts to force her into the marriage.

- A girl who is keen on following fashion trends, which are distinguished by tight and short clothes. Therefore, she gained the disapproval of her fiancé, so he advised her to wear long clothes that are not eye-catching. She replied sarcastically in disapproving manner, saying, "You know it's trendy to wear short clothes. I'll never wear the style that you're telling me to wear. What do you want people to say about me? Then again, why do you want me to dress like this while I was still in the prime of my youth?"

This girl is not afraid that people will accuse her of breaking the traditions of the society related dress code. However, she is afraid that people will accuse her of not following fashion trends. We find that those flying away to gain their freedom may be driven by their eagerness to continue flying that they fall into the trap of extremism that make them prisoners of the concepts of freedom that they seek, forcing them to adopt a modernist behavior to adhere to. They are just like the submissive people who suffer from the rules and laws of the traditional culture. In the last situation, a phrase that has long been repeated by those who conform to traditional culture caught my attention - specifically, "What will people say about me?" However, in this case, it was said by someone who resists that culture. This indicates that both the submissive and the resistant people are subject to a power that imposes a certain kind of behavior. We see that the submissive person submits to traditional powers, while the resistant person is subject to modernist powers that impose modernist behavior on them.

c) Preserving the Status:

Those who swim against the tide seek to resist all types of traditional powers that are imposed on them, in order to maintain and consolidate their social status which they may lose, or at least got shaken, when they submit to traditions and keep eye on shame. Perhaps, in presenting some situations, we can clearly illustrate this:

- An uncle deliberately interferes with his nephew's life and affairs with and without reason, until the nephew was fed up with his uncle's behavior with him. So he waited for the uncle to get involved in one of his affairs and said to him insistently, "Please, uncle! I truly value and cherish you. But I am not young boy anymore. I don't need anyone to interfere with my life and take charge of my affairs. Please, don't interfere again."

This man's objection to his uncle was caused by his uncle interference with his life and directing it without being authorized or delegated to do so. This has led to undermining his status, shaking of his personality, and inability to direct his personal affairs, as there is a reference and authority to which he must refer before doing anything in his life. Therefore, when he stood up firmly to his uncle to prevent him from interfering with his personal affairs again. Accordingly, he reclaimed his status, and started to control and direct his personal affairs, away from any reference or authority.

- A man, of prestigious position, has an elderly relative who lives in a village. Whenever the relative sees the man, he tries to force him to address him with the word (uncle) before his name, and to interact with him on this basis. The man commented, saying, " Do you think I'm still a young boy to dictate to me what to say, and how to interact with people? Look and see who you're talking to!"

This man, who is of prestigious position and status, is not looking for a social status, which he has already obtained it from his prestigious position. It is a status that is recognized by everyone who knows his position. And he didn't do anything that would diminish his status. But it was his relative who tries to diminish his status by making him appear inferior to him in the village, based only on his old age. Thus, the man's response was harsh in order to cement his position in his village, and with this relative.

- A child objects to his parents driving him to school every day and asking the teachers about his academic level. He says, "I don't want anyone to ask about me. My friends make fun of me and call me 'little baby' because my parents ask about me."

Despite the seemingly trivial nature of this situation, it highlights the fact that maintaining one's social status is not limited to a certain age group. In this particular case, a child felt that his status among his peers was being undermined when his parents drove him to school every day and inquired about his academic performance with his teachers. So they started shame him and accusing him of being (a little baby). Therefore, he objected to his parents' behavior with him in order to support his status among his colleagues.

Preserving the status is one of the quests that those who swimmers against the tide try to achieve. And it pushes them to take a stance of resistance against those who abuse them and try to undermine their status.

2) Faces without masks:

By this title, I mean those who resist, neither consciously nor intentionally. Rather, it is more accurate to say that they don't even know that they are resisting. Yet, their behaviors and actions seem resistant, as they go against the socially imposed behaviors and rules. Hence, they are considered resisting people in the eyes of society, while they are not aware of being so.

So in order to avoid being ambiguous and unclear, I'll provide some examples to clarify what is meant. For example, the actions of children are instinctive, spontaneous, and automatic, and completely free from any restrictions in which we keep molding them into, in order for them to become duplicates of us. Unwittingly, their spontaneous actions can be considered acts against the behaviors that we expect from them. Also, the lower classes of society, we see their behavior as if it were a blatant defiant act against the concepts and morals that society imposes on its members, due to their bold and revealing behaviors. However, these classes don't do all of this in defiance of the society that marginalizes them. Rather, they do it because this is their nature on the one hand, and due to the fact that their adherence to these social rules does not add anything to their social capital on the other hand. Therefore, the people categorized under this title are considered unconsciously and unintentionally resistant.

These resistant people can be clearly seen in the lower levels, children, people of similar age, and same-sex individuals, the presence of power is wiped out and fades into a climate of parity and absence of pretense. Hence their practice appears free and spontaneous, unbothered by its occasional appearance of ugliness. It is a natural practice, without any pretense or disguises. Let's get a closer look at those are resisting through their practice in everyday situations:

- In a popular neighborhood, a woman was heard loudly cursing at her son in the street with vulgar language. Her son responded in kind, and the exchange of insults was witnessed and heard by those passing by.

This example clearly reveals the extent to which the lower classes of the society are characterized by their ability to liberate themselves from the restrictions produced by society and by which its individuals and classes are judged.

- In a public setting, a young girl removed her clothes and urinated in the street while her mother assisted her with undressing. The incident occurred in full view of passersby.

This example isn't different from the previous one, except that I would like to add that the lower levels of society seem to be distracted by the worries of everyday life from adhering to the behavioral rules even with their children. In addition, adhering to such behaviors did not add much to their social standing, as they are marginalized and resort to resisting social constraints - if I may say - without fear or concern for their social appearance.

However, the lower classes' non-compliance with social norms is viewed with satisfaction and approval, especially when it comes to children. For example:

- A young child curses another child in the street with vulgar words, encouraged by his mother, who was saying to him with admiration, "Yes! that's how you do it. Good for you, son! I want you to be vulgar and know how to make things right for yourself on your own."

The behavior of the mother and her son can only be understood in the context of the environment they live in, which due to social marginalization, holds the belief that a true man is one who fiercely fights for his rights against the world rather than seeking help or support. Again, when you see a child who shows signs of being able to fight ferociously for their rights in the future, they must be admired and applauded. Just like this child who won the heart and admiration of their mother because they cursed another child with profane words in the street. It is an act that the mother considers a sign of early manhood that will make them qualified to fight ferociously for their rights throughout their life in the future.

But since this form of resistance is encouraged by the parent; there are other forms of child resistance that are met with the parents' disapproval and astonishment of such behavior. Perhaps the following two examples will illustrate this:

- A child was sitting with his family in the presence of some guests to watch a program on television. During the program, a presenter appeared with thick curly hair, so the child comments with apparent innocence, saying, "This woman looks like grandma when she is at home! Her hair is messy just like this." The mother sent a threatening look at him, in front of the guests.

- A child went along with his family that was invited to dinner at some relatives'. After eating dinner, the hostess joked with the child, saying, "What do you think about dinner? How did you find it?" The child replied, "It is very bad. Not yummy." His mother hastily said, "Shame on you, son!" Then she addressed the hostess, saying, "He's just a kid. He doesn't mean it. Thanks so much for the food!"

So, what is the form that we should raise our children on? I see that we are unconsciously teaching them to lie and practice social hypocrisy. I think we are familiarizing them with social dishonesty and hypocrisy, without even realizing it. So we often become dissatisfied with their frankness, or rather their innocence; believing that they should learn to give compliments and become accustomed to concealing the unpleasant aspects of their lives from others. Hence, it's not appropriate for a child to describe his grandmother in such a negative manner in front of others. Similarly, when a child expresses his dissatisfaction with the food served to him, we often feel compelled to teach him to lie and pretend that everything is fine. This unwittingly instills in him the habit of social hypocrisy and dishonesty. We often see children resist authority and social norms without fully understanding the restrictions and traditions placed upon them. Their resistance is pure, sincere, and highlights their innocence, with no need for them to put on any mask.

Resistance also appears among closer age groups or within the same gender groups, where power dynamics are less pronounced; which allows for freer and more resistant behavior. In these situations, individuals can act with indifference towards anyone or anything. To illustrate this, we can present some examples:

-     A group of girls sitting in a cafe smoking hookah, not caring about those around them.

- In the absence of men or any other forms of power in the work environment, women talk freely, frankly, and in a spontaneous way. The content of their speech is also resistant, as they talk about everything and resist everything (the authority of the husband, the harshness of life, the manager... etc.).

- As long as nobody else can hear them, a group of men will talk about sex frankly and expressly, attempting to show off their masculinity and virility.

Thus, each age group or same gender group creates its form of resistance, or rather, their free behavior (attitude) that appears resistant and indifferent to anyone. And this can be seen clearly in, what I've referred to, the erosion of power among them.

II- Resistance: Need vs. Protest

When reading situation about those who are resisting in their everyday life, this question arises; what makes the resisting person go against and reject the traditional culture of his society? He even decides to confront vigorously all the social behaviors and rules that he deems invalid and resists them. Although this could expose him to the loss of much of his earned symbolic capital in the society. So, is it his nature or are there other reasons?

Although this could expose him to the loss of much of his symbolic capital in society. So, is it his nature or are there other reasons? However, resisting traditional culture is not solely motivated by a lack of awareness. In fact, I have observed instances of resistance in highly-educated and cultured individuals whose resistance manifests itself differently in a different for than that of the aforementioned group. These individuals possess a heightened awareness of their society's traditional culture and are attuned to its negative and positive aspects. They are able to critically question certain practices and behaviors that are perceived as shameful or taboo. and in case they are not offered a satisfactory answer, their resistance will be expressed resolutely and with conviction.

However, there are other reasons for resistance that I've also noticed in these situations. This includes the resistance of someone who loses trust in his society, as a result of his inability to find a job that can provide him with the basic necessities of life, for example. This also includes the resistance of those who come back from abroad after completing their education in foreign countries or working there. They return to reject the culture of their society and promote a more modernist Western culture in their view.

So there are other reasons that can be added to the nature of the resisting person's personality, which can reveal what makes him go against the traditional culture of his society. And this indicates that resistance is a need for resisting people as a natural result of a various range of reasons that lead to their resistance. Since they are people who live their lives with faces that reject the traditional powers, falsehoods and masks in the society. Perhaps, by presenting some of the expressions said by some of the resisting people, we can understand such situation:

- I am not doing anything wrong.

- I'm old enough.

- I want to live my life.

- I don't care about anyone.

- Everybody should mind their business.

- I'm free.

These expressions reveal the nature of the resisting people who can articulate the idea that I sought to explain, which is the idea of "need" that I referred to.

However, when people resist the traditional culture of their society, society doesn't always tolerate it silently. Instead, the society often confronts and protests against such behavior, viewing it as a challenge to the culture that it imposes on its individuals and groups. The following situations from the everyday life reveal the society's protest against the resisting people:

- A rural woman divorced (Khula) her husband because of his mistreatment and abuse of her. Yet, she faced the alienation of her family and neighbors, and the concern of her female colleagues. When a young man proposed to marry her daughter, his father strongly rejected this marriage, arguing, "Couldn't you find another girl other than this one? Her mother is going head-to-head with men. You know what they say, son. Like mother, like daughter!"

Thus, the father's attitude towards this marriage clearly expressed the society's rejection of this woman's behavior, despite the fact that she exercised a legal right guaranteed to her by laws in place. However, her behavior was rejected by the members of society, who questioned her conduct and extended their suspicions to her daughter's behavior as well. They based their assumptions on popular proverbs that portrayed daughters as mirrors of their mothers.

- A girl who defied her family and worked in the cinema industry. So her family disowned her, and refused to interact with her, despite her repeated attempts to appease them.

A family's attitude towards their daughter, who became a professional film actress, is a reflection of the society's unforgiving attitude towards wrongdoing, no matter how long ago it occurred.

This was how the society protested against some of its members who resist its traditional culture, which is imposed on its individuals and group by force. But what will the resisting people do? Will they overcome the protest of the society and move forward towards the resistance? Or return to the ranks of the submissives and attempt to improve their image in front of society, which was distorted by their resistance? Or do they have a third solution? This is what the next pages will reveal.

III- Resistance Strategies:

I won't go into the details of the strategy and its significance since I already covered it in the previous chapter. However, I would like to bring up a point that was discussed earlier. Society provides an individual with symbolic capital as long as they conform to the traditions and cultural values of that society. The individual resorts to the strategy when a crisis or a clash occurs between a practice and the rule in order to find harmony between them. Therefore, the core principle of the submission strategy revolves around the question of how individuals should behave in the presence of others. The individual's top priority within this strategy is to ensure that his behavior aligns with the expectations of society, so as to preserve his symbolic capital.

My discussion in this section is about the other side of that strategy, which is the "Resistance Strategy". The society that rewards the submissive person with symbolic capital based on the extent of his conformity to its traditions and cultural values, is the same one that strips the resisting person of his symbolic capital when his resists those traditions and values. When the society responds to resistance with rejection, indignation, and protest, the resisting individual needs to find a strategy to reconcile his needs with society's reaction and shock towards his deviation from tradition. Hence, a strategy is created for the resisting people who are keen to please the society.

Here, we need to know the difference between the two types of resisting people. The first type is the one who resists the traditional culture of his society, relying on defiance and confrontation with the various social powers. This type does not care much about their symbolic capital, and therefore they don't need a strategy to conform to the society.

The second type of resistance is also characterized by their defiance against social norms, but unlike the first type, these individuals are concerned with maintaining their symbolic capital within society. Therefore, this type needs a strategy that allows them to find a sense of compatibility between their resistance and the socially imposed rules, in order to preserve their status and reputation within the community. This section revolves around this type.

By reviewing the everyday situations, we can conclude that the resistance strategy into two integral forms that complement each other, namely;

1. The Disguise Strategy.

2. The Justification and Value Addition Strategy.

3. The Language Strategy

By their integration, I mean that the resisting person resorts to disguising and hiding from the eyes of society in order to exercise his resistance freely, And in case the society knows the nature of his practice, the resisting person will resort to justifying his practices and adding value to them. The following is a detailed discussion of the two strategies:

1)   The Disguise Strategy:

The core principle of this strategy is based on the following question; how do I practice resistance without anyone seeing me? The answer to this question shapes the disguise strategy. As the ultimate concern of the resisting person here is wanting the eyes and minds of the society and its members to remain oblivious to his resistance, in order for him to continue gaining their approval and appreciation. Let's view some everyday situations to see the ways of the resisting people use to disguise and hide from view:

- A girl wanted to go on a trip with her classmates and colleagues at the university, but her father refused because he was concerned that she would return late at night, which could result in negative comments from their neighbors and lead to gossip and criticism. So the girl proposed a solution to her father, which he found acceptable, and he allowed her to go on the trip. Her solution was to stay at her aunt's who lived in another neighborhood after the trip ends, and return home the next day after her lectures at the university, which was her usual time for returning. This way, nobody would pay attention to her and she would avoid the potential gossip and criticism from the neighbors.

Thus, this girl created a disguising strategy that enabled her to live her life without being exposed to anyone's sharp tongues or denunciation. Spending the night at her aunt's, who lives in another neighborhood and another district, was a successful solution that enabled her to go on her trip with her colleagues and enjoy it, without harming her reputation in front of her neighbors. This solution also satisfied her father, because it guarantees that neither his family nor his daughter will be exposed to gossip. As for her aunt's neighbors, it will be fine because they don't know the girl. Therefore, no one will pay attention to her or ask about her. So the girl, with her disguising strategy, has managed to combine enjoying the trip, while preserving her image and that of her family in front of neighbors and acquaintances.

- A mother refuses to let her daughter wear a very tight top, arguing that she fears the father's reaction, saying, "You can't leave the house like this. If your father saw you like this, it's going to be a big trouble for us. The top is very tight. Wear a jacket over it." Her daughter replied, "I don't want to wear a jacket on it. This's trendy now, and the jacket will cover it and it won't be visible." The mother replied decisively, "Wear the jacket, or else you won't go out." The younger sister confided to the eldest the solution, saying, "Come on, stupid girl! Go out with the jacket in front of Mum, and then take it off at the staircase. When you come back at night, put it on before you ring the bell, because Dad will be home then."

The younger sister offered a solution or strategy that helped her eldest sister to overcome the dilemma of her desire to wear whatever clothes she wanted while facing her mother's refusal due to her fear of the father's reaction. This solution is for her to do whatever she wants away from the authority imposed on her by her mother and father, or rather performing disguised resistance.

- A woman from the middle class, who was pushed by the lack of money to work in order to improve her income and standard of living, so she worked as a sales representative. She used to go to various government authorities and schools to display her goods to the employees, including household supplies, clothes, and perfumes. But she was afraid that someone would recognize her and tell her family or neighbors. So she resorted to changing her name and wearing a face veil (Niqab). When she finishes her work, she returns to her home and her normal life by taking off the veil, which no one has seen her wear.

The woman in this example was compelled to conceal and disguise herself from society because of its unfavorable attitude towards women who work as sales representatives. This necessitated her disguise in order to maintain her own and her family's status, as they belonged to the middle class which held a certain perception about the nature of such work. This approach allowed her to keep her surroundings unaffected while also improving her income and preserving her status with the disguise.

There are numerous examples of individuals resorting to various methods of disguise in everyday life to carry out their practices away from society. For instance:

- A family turns off the TV due to the death of one of their close neighbors. The son of the family tries to turn on the TV because he has been watching a series, and the mother replies to him in disapproval, "Shame on you, son! What will people say about us? Their door is next to our door." The son makes an agreement with his mother so that he can turn on the TV and lower its volume to a degree that no one outside the room can hear. So if the doorbell rang, the family would rush to turn off the TV first, then open the door.

- A girl who works as a housemaid without her family knowing. On her day off, she took a means of transportation with one of her relatives to go to a public park for a picnic. While they were travelling, she saw her employer in the means of transportation. So the girl hid her face with her hand, and turned it to the other side so that she would not meet her employer's eyes and have a discussion that would reveal the truth about her.

- A woman who was forced by her husband to wear a niqab found a way to resist his control when she traveled alone to visit her family in her village. During these trips, she would remove the niqab and reveal her face, allowing herself to interact with the people in her village without the veil. When she returns to her husband, she wears the niqab before meeting him.

- A girl puts on makeup with her friends at the university, and wipes it off with a tissue when she returns home before her family sees her.

- A child wants to do some unpleasant things, like messing with his mother's hand bag, or messing with some things in the house. In order not to get scolded, he directs his younger brother and incites him to act instead. And when his brother brings whatever he wants, they play with them together.

- Two women leave a nightclub early in the morning, and at the outer gate of the nightclub, each of them wears a black Abaya and veil, then gets into a taxi and leaves.

These are some of the practices, and many others, that the resisting people adopt, using some tricks and strategies that help them disguise in order to do whatever they like without the other knowing. It reminds me of (the cloak of invisibility), which is legend that came to us from the cultural heritage. It was used to conceal the wearer and enable him to do anything away from the eyes of others. This cloak, or rather (the strategy of disguise), represents the absence of power that makes them feel that no one can see them, and thus make them reassured when they undertake any action, or rather resistance.

But what will happen if this cloak ceased to work? Or in other words, what if others discover the practices that the resisting people are concealing? The answer to this question leads us to the second form of the resistance strategy, which is:

2- The Justification and Value Addition Strategy:

Musa Al-Husseini defines justification as "the tendency to fabricate imaginary justifications to excuse wrong behavior" (Musa Al-Husseini, p. 156). This meaning is exactly what the resisting person does; as he resorts to justifying his actions due to his inability to confront others with them. The everyday situations are full of practices that the resisting person justify to become impeccable practices:

- As a man witnessed a young man catcalling some girls on the street, he admonished him, "Shame on you, son! They are like your sisters." The young man replies to him, "They deserve to that. Don't you see what they are wearing and what they do to themselves? If they do not like it, they should wear a long veil (Khemar), sit at home and respect themselves."

This example illustrates the justification strategy that the resisting person resorts to when his practice becomes clear to others. This young man didn't apologize to the man or the girls for the act of cat calling that he did, but resorted to justification to excuse his wrong behavior and prove that the wrongdoer in this situation is the girls because of their behavior and appearance.

- A girl justifies to her classmate, who saw her talking to a colleague of theirs at the university in private, saying, "I don't want you to get a wrong idea about me talking to him. I was just taking the lectures I missed from him. As you saw, I was speaking to him politely, and there was a distance between me and him."

The girl was afraid that her classmate would misunderstand her, so she felt compelled to justify her conversation with a young man at the university. In her defense, she explained two things. First, the reason for the conversation was to take lectures from him. The second is the way she stood while she talked to him (was speaking to him politely, and there was a distance between me and him). In doing so, she makes her practice sound proper.

Just as the resisting person resorts to a strategy by which he justifies his actions to others with the intention of gaining recognition, he also resorts to another strategy to add value to his actions for the same reason, which is to gain recognition for his actions. Adding value to a behavior transforms it from shameful behavior to praised behavior that must be taken care of. The following situations will reveal this:

- A group of middle school teachers let the students cheat in the exam classrooms. However, when another teacher wanted to control the classroom and refuse to let them cheat, one of these teachers told him, "What are you doing? Isn't it already bad enough for people?" The teacher replied, "That's how exams should go. Not like what you're doing!" So, he said to him, "What we do is part of our duty. We appreciate the efforts of families, and we must be kind to the students, and feel the suffering of the parents. They shouldn't find their children failed their exams after paying all these expenses. That's so wrong (Haram!)"

This is the value bestowed on cheating transformed it from fraud and unworthy act into duty, kindness, and alleviation of suffering. Thus, the person who practices this value is then transformed into a hero, chivalrous person who is considerate of the suffering of others.

- A female gynecologist was asked about her opinion regarding surgical procedures that aim to restore virginity for girls. The doctor replied, "What about it? I do these procedures. You must know that I'm an advocate for covering shortcomings and sins in every aspect of life. God commanded us to so."

Thus, falsehood and deceit turned into a cover-up, and the person in charge of doing them is an executor of God's command and will.

- An employee who posed as her fellow employee to attend a training course instead of her to help her obtain a financial return, in return for the former taking part from the latter's financial return. When the first employee came back after the end of the course and told her colleagues what she had done in place of her colleague, she won everyone's admiration. One colleague said to her, "By God, you are a wicked one! What a badass! You are fearless. You didn't worry that someone would recognize you there!"

This example is not much different from the previous one, except that falsehood and deceit have made someone (badass) and (fearless), and therefore their practice deserves to be praised.

Thus, we can observe that the resisting person employs a variety of strategies to achieve their goals while maintaining their symbolic capital in society. This includes hiding from view at times, justifying actions that may not be accepted by society at other times, and even adding positive values to those actions in order to legitimize them. These tactics serve as tools for the resisting person to attain their desires while simultaneously preserving their status and reputation in society.

But what about the language of the resisting person, which is part of his strategy? This is what I will try to explain in the following lines.

3- The Language strategy:

The language of the resisting person is characterized by decisiveness and defiance. It is also a bold language that can address all topics, even those that one considered taboos, according to the concepts of traditional culture.

But if this is the language of the resisting person, then what about the resisting person who does not have the ability to explicitly resist in the face of the power imposed on him socially? What is the nature of his language? Is it different from the language of the resisting who confronts the traditional culture explicitly? Of course, it is a language that's different from the language of the outspoken resisting person. It's distinguished by its lack of both decisiveness or defiance. Rather, this person creates his own linguistic strategy, so to speak, through which he resists the powers imposed on him.

By reflecting on the everyday situations, we can identify two forms of this strategy: The verbal resistance and mumbling as a means of resistance.

(A) The Verbal Resistance:

It is verbal resistance that does not go beyond the tongue, and doesn't come into effect. This resistance is represented in the form of a wish that the person wishes to achieve, or a fantasy that he wants to achieve it, but is unable to achieve it because of the powers surrounding him. Hence, his resistance is limited to what I called "verbal resistance." The following situations demonstrate this type of resistance:

- An employee arrived late for work, and his manager reprimanded him in front of his colleagues, saying, "If this happened again, I will not have mercy on you. Where do you think you are working?" The employee didn't utter a single word to defend himself in front of his boss. But after the manager left, the employee revolted in front of his colleagues, saying, "Who does he think himself is to talk to me in this way? I swear I won't remain silent if he talks to me this way again. And he will know what's the deal then!"

- A young man fakes false romantic relationships in front of his friends. And in order to prove the validity of his claims to them, he spoke in front of them on his mobile phone with one of his girlfriends. While talking to her, his phone suddenly rang. His colleagues laughed at him.

Thus, the resistance of this type of people served as a wish they wanted to fulfill. However, they failed to actually achieve it. Therefore, they did the act of resistance, though not in the face of the powers they should have resisted.

(B) Mumbling as a Means of Resistance:

The language strategy of some resisting people takes the shape of mumbling. Mumbling linguistically means saying what one cannot reveal in the presence of others in the form of incomprehensible words. This meaning can be clearly see in everyday situations. For example:

-       A mother admonishes her young son for playing with a ball at home. So when she hits him and takes the ball from him, he mumbles some incomprehensible words. When the mother asked him harshly, "What did you say, boy?" He replied to her, saying, "I didn't say anything."

-       - An old man confronts a young man in the street who was catcalling a girl, saying to him, "Shame, my son! She is like your sister. Would you like it if someone catcalls your sister?" The young man replied, denouncing his interference, "Why don't you mind your business! Leave me alone." The man then fell silent and mumbled with a low voice, "When did we sink to this low?" The young man kept glaring at him.

-       A manager reprimands an employee for his negligence at work, and after he stopped reprimanding him, he ordered him to go to his office to complete the rest of his work. So the employee left while mumbling some incomprehensible words to express his dismay.

Thus, the mumbling was used to express one of the two forms that the resisting people resort to express their desire for resistance, when they can't find another way except through language.

Conclusion

This study has led to the conclusion that a person's behavior and practices are shaped by the type of power that governs them, whether it is imposed by individuals or instilled through cultural upbringing. The manner in which a person exercises this power can be either forceful or habitual. The practice of submission, for example, is closely linked to the symbolic capital that society grants to the individual, thus giving him social strength and acceptance. As a result, others become the main judges of the individual's behavior. Given this situation, the individual can increase their social status and gain the support of others by simply conforming to their expectations and submitting to their judgment. Thus, their sense of self becomes a collective self that aligns and harmonizes with the group, and they behave in ways that match those of others, avoiding anything that might mark them as abnormal or out of sync. This is because any such deviation weakens their social standing and undermines the symbolic capital they have worked to accrue, diminishing their social power and status.

Perhaps the fear of losing social power and status is what drives the self to adopt strategies to maintain its image and status in society. This is why we see individuals submitting or resisting secretly or creating multiple areas in which their practices can differ and multiply. They transition among such practices with great skill and heightened awareness, reflecting their understanding of the culture surrounding them. As such, it should come as no surprise that the self engages in modernist practices within its own social sphere with confidence and enthusiasm, without necessarily disclosing its adherence to traditionalism. Similarly, the same self may proudly perform traditional practices within its own social sphere, without acknowledging any conflict with its modernist tendencies, and without perceiving any contradiction between the two. This social duality compels us to act and practice in a way that makes it seem as though someone is always watching and judging us. Consequently, we end up leading multiple lives, leading to a loss of our identity. (Alain Touraine, 1997, p. 38).

Based on the aforementioned, I can also say that the obsession with social evaluation of our behavior has become a power or an authority, that imposes on us our practices and determines its nature. Reflecting on this issue, I can't help but wonder what would happen if we no longer had anyone to observe and inspect our behavior, and if we relinquished the need for supervisors over our actions. As a result, the need for external assessments or social sanctions imposed on those who violate the values and traditions of society would no longer exist. Will the proper behaviors disappear from our lives at that time? Or will we try to reinstate the powers that were once imposed on us, in order to regain their influence and give ourselves a sense of purpose once more? Is it acceptable to do the right thing publicly and then privately discard that act? This with no doubt creates a strange and contradictory duality. I think we are in dire need of another power, a power of a special kind, a power that can work in secret and in public and makes us abstain from doing shameful behaviors, not because someone sees us, but rather because they are not consistent with what we believe in terms of principles and values, and are not consistent with what we want to be, not what others want us to be. I believe that the only power that can create an atmosphere of consistency is one that resides in our conscience. Dear conscience, How much we miss you. We are looking for you. May you have power over us, day and night. Captivate us. Control us. With you, shame is corrupted, and by your corruption, shame will occur and multiply.

✳✳✳

9 798340 539854